the
Dynamic
CLASSROOM

ENGAGING STUDENTS
in HIGHER EDUCATION

Edited by Catherine Black

Atwood Publishing
Madison, WI

The Dynamic Classroom: Engaging Students in Higher Education
Edited by Catherine Black

ISBN: 978-1-891859-82-3
© Atwood Publishing, 2010
Madison, WI
www.atwoodpublishing.com

Cover design by Tamara Dever, TLC Graphics, www.tlcgraphics.com
Cover illustration by Susan Tolonen, www.susantolonen.com

Library of Congress Cataloging-in-Publication Data

The dynamic classroom : engaging students in higher education / edited
by Catherine Black.
    p. cm.
  ISBN 978-1-891859-82-3 (pb)
  1. Education, Higher. 2. Education, Higher—Aims and objectives. 3.
College teaching. I. Black, Catherine, 1954-
  LB2322.2.D96 2010
  378.1'7—dc22

                                        2010019427

Contents

Preface

Education is not for spectators. Every educator wants to see his or her students participate willingly and actively in the process of learning. The question is how best to achieve that goal. The center of the professional dialogue in this area has shifted: from communication to engagement. Experts in higher education recognize that even with successful communication from teachers, students still often fail to participate. Thus the critical issue at hand has undergone a subtle but important transition from "getting through to students" to "getting students to actively engage." The papers in *The Dynamic Classroom* reflect this central shift in the educational focus as they approach the vital topic of student engagement from multiple different angles, with a special interest in the use of new technologies.

Our objective in putting together the papers for *The Dynamic Classroom: Engaging Students in Higher Education* is to help faculty members and teachers transform students from passive to active learners. Therefore, the purpose of this book is fourfold, as represented in the four parts of the book: first, we prepare the ground for active participation; second, we look at engagement in a variety of settings; third, we leave the more conventional classroom to explore engagement in virtual or hybrid classrooms; and fourth, we examine how to assess online and in-class participation. It is important to note that all the articles for this book have been commissioned. By calling on the expertise of colleagues and researchers in a broad range of fields (psychology, biology, languages, business, and education), as well as educational developers, I knew the articles would vary in style and length, but would all focus on engagement. Some are anchored in theory, others are more practically based, but they all demonstrate genuine concern for engaging students more in their learning process.

Each article can be read separately; the reader will find that within each part, the articles complement each other, and there is a deliberate path from the first to the last part.

In Part One, *Preparing the Ground for Engaging Students*, the reader will have to reflect on what precludes engagement: E. Wood looks at the questions we tend to ask in the classroom, J. A. Specht focuses on students with learning disabilities who tend to be forgotten when engagement is concerned, and E. Biktimirov proposes the use of mind mapping techniques to help students understand difficult concepts and apply them in discussion.

In Part Two, *Engaging Students in a Variety of Settings*, two university professors and an educational developer look at the environment itself: K. Cawsey tells us how to use the "dreaded pause" in a small- to medium-sized classroom, M. Atkinson demystifies the extra large classroom as a particularly passive type of environment by offering some tips and activities, and J. McDonald defines the inquiry circle by presenting its five principles and proposing some activities that will engage students in that type of setting.

In Part Three, *Engaging Students with New Technologies*, the reader moves to the virtual classroom. This part is the largest of the book because the new technologies are part of students' reality. More and more, instructors feel "the need for speed" as the millennium students, who grew up with technology, expect their instructors to use it in class. M. Crosslin helps the not-so-computer-savvy instructor choose between two different platforms, blogging or discussion boards, to engage the students in effective participation. M. Anderson advocates LiveJournal as an alternative technique to traditional journaling to engage students to be more reflective. Through four cases studies she illustrates her point and demonstrates students' growth, self-reflection, and the creation of a unique community. M. Rowinsky-Geurts also looks at these aspects with the use of portfolios in the final part. M. L. Ripley shows that online discussions will foster more contact with students than in a regular classroom, providing three cardinal rules are applied. E. Meyer and colleagues promote the electronic portfolio from kindergarten to grade 12 and in higher education as a way of extending classroom spaces and being more inclusive. T. Haffie offers the most thorough article on "Clickers." He presents "broad-collecting"—as he prefers to call it—in a very clear manner, then takes the reader through a series of practical examples showing their pedagogical benefits. Definitely a must read! In the last article of Part Three, D. Yearwood provides the reader with an interesting article on podcasting. In his article, not only does he gives a history of this new way of disseminating information, but he also provides the reader with an almost exhaustive list of the technical tools one needs to prepare a podcast. But what is certainly the most important aspect of this article is the author's concern that podcasting should be used by instructors who know the what, why, when, and for whom the technology will be used to really engage students and enhance their learning.

In Part Four, *Assessing Students' Engagement*, we look at assessment methods. Even though introducing new online approaches and teaching strategies is always exciting, the instructors are often confronted with the task of assessing students' engagement or participation. It is often difficult to do so for in-class courses, but it is particularly difficult for online courses. D. Stockley and W. Freeman insist that transparency is vital to the process, so both students and instructors are clear about what engagement through participation entails. They demonstrate that when participation is assessed, it shows students that their contributions are valued, and that contributes to the success of the course. Assessing participation fosters engagement in online courses. But it also works in class, if portfolios are used, as M. Rowinsky-Geurts demonstrates in the last article of the collection. By offering the students the tools (formal rubric) for formative assessment of their work and of their peers, students' interest augments and fosters a sense of community where everyone feels comfortable expressing their points of view and sharing positively with others.

Finally, at the end of the book, we have added a short section, "For Further Reflection and Action," in which instructors can find new ideas to try in their classes.

Engaging students through active participation is certainly one of the most difficult tasks to trigger, nurture, stimulate, and assess. This is what this book is all about. As the editor, I believe this collection of articles gives some insight on this elusive notion called engagement. The key is to know what questions to ask, to know our learners, to familiarize ourselves with approaches and new technologies in class or online. I hope these articles have given the reader the urge not only to try something different, but to do it while being more informed.

I would like to thank Atwood Publishing for making this book possible and all the contributors for their enthusiasm and commitment to bringing this project to life.

Catherine Black

Part One

Preparing the Ground for Engaging Students

It Is Yours for the Asking

Using Questioning to Promote Discussion in the Classroom

Eileen Wood
Wilfrid Laurier University

INTRODUCTION

What could be more natural than engaging students by asking a question? After all, questions are a pervasive and familiar part of our everyday interactions. We use questions to greet people, gain information, and share our ideas, feelings, hopes, and concerns. Given the heavy reliance on questions as a form of communication, it would seem sensible that questioning would be an easy, accessible, and effective way to encourage interaction and thinking within the classroom. Then why is it that asking questions often yields long, empty pauses, averted eye contact, quizzical looks, and awkwardness instead of engagement?

There are several reasons why the natural flow of questions and answers experienced in everyday exchanges doesn't translate easily to the classroom setting. Many of the problems with introducing questioning as a forum for promoting discussion arise as a function of the "structure" of classrooms. Even in well-designed, supportive classroom environments, there is a built-in power differential with instructors at the top of the hierarchy. Instructors have expectations when asking questions, and students know that. Students also know that they will be evaluated both by their instructor and their peers when and if they answer questions (McKeachie and Svinicki 2006; Myers et al. 2007; Weaver and Qi 2005). In addition, the social structure of classrooms differs from typical day-to-day social interactions. Typical social exchanges occur in one-to-one or small group contexts where people know one another. In classrooms, there are often a great number of people and many, if not all, may be relative strangers. Finally, the types of questions asked in higher education contexts typically differ from the kinds of questions experienced in casual conversation. Indeed, even within educational environments, the types of questions experienced vary, especially as students move through the grades. Specifically, questioning in grade school is more likely to be lower order, involving a right or wrong response, whereas the kinds of questions found in higher education contexts are those that promote critical thinking, inquiry, and elaboration. These questions tend to be more open and allow for more than one "correct" response. This means that students have to not only acquire new knowledge in their courses but also learn how to answer critical thinking questions. Answers to higher-order questions are predicated on an expectation of assumed knowledge. This knowledge is typically acquired through readings, lectures, or prior classroom discussions. In order to answer these questions, students need to be prepared for classes as well as for the types of questions they need to answer. Therefore, answering questions is a risky and challenging behavior for many students and may present a potential cost in terms of personal self-esteem as well as achieving educational goals (Karabenick 1994; McKeachie and Svinicki 2006). It is no surprise then that attempts to introduce questioning often result in silence rather than discussion.

Overcoming these structural challenges requires expertise on the part of the instructor and training for students. This article explores the underpinnings of questions, the demands we place on students, and the role of the instructor in making questioning a comfortable and accessible format within the classroom context.

WHAT AM I ASKING?

Not all questions are equal. Some questions require considerably more skill, knowledge, and planning in order to generate a response. The variation in cognitive demands across different types of questions has been a focal point of research for some time. Much of the research examining questions divides questions into two types: higher-order and lower-order questions. Lower-order questions typically require simple access to existing information. These are generally represented by factual level questions, such as remembering a specific fact, term, date, formula, and so on. Higher-order questions require the learner to go beyond the information given. That is, the student is required to access prior knowledge and then manipulate or elaborate on that information in new or unique ways (Willoughby et al. 2000; Wood et al. 1999). For example, when we ask students to compare and contrast, they must first access the two relevant areas and then systematically search the information in each of the two domains for things that might be similar or different. This requires them to consider, accept, and reject decisions about the material they know—a considerably more challenging cognitive task than simply remembering material. Understanding the cognitive operations we expect of students is a first step in understanding when we should or should not use a question in the classroom and why students may or may not answer.

UNDERSTANDING THE COGNITIVE DEMANDS IN THE QUESTIONS ASKED

Over sixty years ago, Bloom (1956) proposed a taxonomy of six cognitive objectives that can be used to discriminate among lower- and higher-order cognitive demands. This taxonomy serves as a good source for understanding the kinds of questions that can be asked and the cognitive demands we are asking of our students. Similar to the lower-order cognitive operations identified earlier, the lowest levels on the taxonomy are represented by objectives that include basic recall of information or knowledge and fundamental comprehension. More advanced items in the taxonomy are consistent with higher-order skills, including comprehension, application, analysis, synthesis, and evaluation. The increasingly higher levels of the taxonomy presuppose all of the skills of the preceding elements of the taxonomy.

Questions consistent with basic recall, knowledge, and comprehension demands typically presume the presence of one correct answer. These questions require minimal or no manipulation or elaboration of information (e.g., "Who was . . .?" or "In what year did . . .?"). The remaining objectives are characterized by questions that require the student to go beyond the information given.

Specifically, questions matching the application level require students to extract general principles in order for these principles to be generalized and applied to unfamiliar domains (Bloom, Hastings, and Madaus 1971). These types of questions invite the student to apply information in a new and novel way, for example, by applying the information to a new context (e.g., "Where would you see an application of . . . in every day life?").

Questions at the analysis level require students to identify underlying assumptions, patterns, or structures. These assumptions can be pre-

13

sented explicitly, but more likely involve inferred values, arguments, and even the form of the presentation (poem, speech, experiment, etc.) may be used to extract underlying assumptions. These questions require students to delve into materials to find out what the "real" message is. (e.g., "What are the fundamental tenets of . . .?" "What would logically follow from . . .?" "What experimental evidence supports . . . point of view?" See Bloom, Hastings, and Madaus 1971.)

While application and analysis involve taking information "apart" to understand the components, synthesis involves being able to collate information and generate something new (e.g., "Based on x, y, and z, can you generate an hypothesis/solution . . .?"). Evaluation-level questions further require students to critically support their own judgments or ideas (e.g., "What evidence would you use to support . . .?" "Explain and identify why you support . . .?"See Bloom, Hastings and Madaus 1971.)

Although Bloom believed that each of these objectives represented increasingly higher demands, most researchers group the objectives into the two categories of lower- and higher-order demands with the understanding that the various higher-order questions reflect qualitatively different demands from one another. Knowing that there are different types of questions and that different questions require students to engage in different cognitive operations is critical when planning to use questions for discussion.

PLANNING TO ASK QUESTIONS

Clearly, questioning does not just "happen," questions need to be planned. Good instructors spend a significant amount of time researching, planning, verifying, and perfecting the accuracy and relevancy of the materials they prepare for their students. This same level of care for precision and accuracy needs to be applied to the questions used in the classroom. Just as we plan our tests to match the material we have covered in our courses, so must our questions match the objectives for the course and the level of preparation of the student. There are no "bad" questions, but there are incorrect and poor uses of questions. To understand how best to use questions consider the following points:

1. Matching Questions and Objectives.
Questions need to match the goals for the day. The topic and/or the objectives of the course need to be reflected in the types of questions posed. For example, if your course objective is to gain an understanding of the

theoretical underpinnings of the work of an important figure in the area (e.g., Jean Piaget), you need to use questions that encourage critical thinking (analysis, synthesis, etc.). Quizzes, exercises, and exams also need to reflect this level of thinking (i.e., the exam would not be based on fact-level questions such as "What are Piaget's stages?").

2. There Are No "Bad" Questions.

There is a misconception among some instructors that some questions are "good" and others "bad," or at least that some questions are better than others. Specifically, the belief is that lower-level, factual questions are not "good" and higher-order questions are "good." Any well-phrased question is an acceptable and useful learning tool, but the function of the question and the impact of the question vary.

Lower-level, factual questions typically require one word or short phrase answers. They also reflect only what is found in the text, reading, or lecture materials. These types of questions are critical for determining what students understand and can recall, but they do nothing to further discussion. So are they bad? The answer is no. However, these questions can be a nonstarter or stop an ongoing discussion if not used effectively, as students will be encouraged to generate that one, short, correct reply and be done.

3. Effectively Using Lower-Order Questions.

The tricks in using lower-order questions in discussions are to minimize their use, to use them primarily as starters or checks for accuracy in information, and to use them predictably.

For example, before launching into a discussion, you can use factual questions as a check to make sure that everyone shares the same correct understanding of the facts needed for the discussion. One way to do this might be to have a standard routine where a set number of lower-order questions (e.g., five to ten) are asked. Be explicit. Tell students that this is the routine and stick to it. Going through the questions should be quick. Following the exchange, the instructor should review the correct and incorrect responses. Incorrect responses can be used as a point of entry for discussion—for example, "Explain why option 'b' could not be the right answer?"

Interesting variations of this opening exercise could include using multiple choice alternatives, perhaps accentuated with the use of new computer technologies (such as where students can select answers using clickers and the instructor can show how many students selected each option, see the article on broadcollecting near the end of this book for more information on these technologies) or more traditional procedures where students can give a show of hands. You might want to have students shout out their answers together so that one voice is not standing out. Alternatively, questions can be given in advance. It is also possible to call on individual students; however, this can be perceived as intimidating for some students.

Summary of the Pros for Lower-order Questions:
- They ensure a general shared knowledge base and allow for quick evaluation or correction for missing or erroneous information.
- They provide a brief review of the material, which encourages students to search their prior knowledge and gears them for further learning.
- Some students, especially shy ones or ones with challenges such as learning English as a second language (ESL), might benefit from clear questions that permit an answer that is easier to express.

The goal is to move beyond factual-level questions quickly and begin to introduce the higher-level questions. If used well, lower-order questions can be used as a springboard or corrective measure to facilitate discussion.

4. Effectively Using Higher-order Questions.

As discussed earlier, being prepared is a key part of using higher-order questions. Instructors need to be able to answer the following question, "Why am I asking questions?" The obvious answer is that the instructor wants to encourage discussion, but there is more to it than that. Using higher-order questions assumes that the instructor wants students to think critically, to evaluate information, synthesize, and apply newly acquired ideas (Özerk 2001). The first step in this process is knowing the questions to ask. Instructors need to be familiar with a variety of questions reflecting the different demands described earlier in Bloom's taxonomy. Both King (1995a; 1995b) and Wisher and Graesser (2006) have mapped out simple tables of question stems with the corresponding cognitive demands identified for each question stem. For example, the four stems shown in Table 1 represent two of sixteen stems identified by King (1995a, 14; 1995b, 28) and two of eighteen stems identified by Wisher and

QUESTION STEM	COGNITIVE TASK
"What is the significance of ...?"	"Analysis ... inference" (King, 1995a & b)
"What do you think causes ...? Why?"	"Analysis ... support an argument" (King, 1995a & b)
"How would you rate X?"	Evaluation — "judgmental" (Wisher & Graesser, 2006)
"What concept or claim can be inferred from (a static or active pattern of data)?"	Synthesis/"interpretation" (Wisher & Graesser, 2006)

Table 1

Graesser (2006, 219). Having access to stems such as these, either by generating your own or referring to these established ones, is a first step in planning the discussion. By practicing the construction and use of these stems, you will be more effective, diverse, and efficient in guiding discussion through questioning.

It is handy to keep a list of question stems available while conducting your class. This allows you ready access to question types so that you can flexibly move from one question to another as the discussion emerges.

THE QUESTIONS ARE READY. NOW WHAT?

Setting the Environment

As mentioned earlier, the classroom environment can support or disable the potential for discussion following questioning. Environments that can maximize the probability of discussion are those that are noncompetitive, supportive, affirming, and student centered (Greeson 1988; Karabenick 1994; Myers et al. 2007). Competitive environments focus on right and wrong answers and on who is getting right answers. Supportive environments move the focus to the tasks of learning and building motivation and excitement about learning. Instructors can facilitate this by stating that their goal in asking questions is to improve students desire to learn and by showing engagement, excitement, and interest in the ideas offered by students (Good et al. 1987; Karabenick 1994). Instructors can create a message of support by clearly acknowledging and affirming students' answers to questions (e.g., "That's a great idea" and "I like how you have put the . . . and . . . together") (Myers et al. 2007).

Awaiting the Answer

The question has been posed. You wait. Nothing is happening. You begin to panic. As noted in "The Dreaded Pause" (in Cawsey, Part Two, above) silence should be expected. If you ask students a higher-order question, you are challenging them and placing high demands on their thinking. They need time to think (McKeachie and Svinicki 2006). Ten seconds is not an unreasonable amount of time to wait. Sometimes it may help some students if you ask them to jot down a few points and then give them thirty seconds to jot down their answers. That way all students will have a chance to think, and more students will be prepared to answer your question (Purdy 2008). In addition, the answers might be better articulated than is sometimes the case with quick, spontaneous outbursts.

Once the students begin to talk, the instructor must listen. Recall that higher-order questions are open ended (Cazden 2001; Skidmore, Perez-Parent, and Arnfield 2003) and allow for more than one interpretation or answer. Students may generate entirely different responses than those anticipated by the instructor. Instructors need to allow themselves time to consider the students' answers and to redirect their questions if needed.

Summary of the Pros for Higher-order Questions:
- They encourage more meaningful learning by making students access their prior knowledge and engage in deeper processing.
- They can promote more active learning as students are required to go beyond the information given to generate an answer (Wood et al. 1999).
- They encourage greater discussion and diversity in responses (Cazden 2001; Purdy 2008).
- They promote the critical thinking necessary to achieve the goals of higher education.

Cultural Differences to Keep in Mind

It is important to be sensitive to cultural differences that might inhibit interaction when questions are used to promote discussion. In some cultures, students are taught that challenging, arguing, or questioning instructors or peers in their class is inappropriate. To avoid problems, it is a good idea to establish classroom "rules" and expectations at the outset and regularly revisit these rules throughout the course. These rules should specify that it is acceptable for students to question and offer alternative viewpoints. It might also be necessary to have a one-on-one chat with some students to ensure that they understand these expectations if there is continued nonparticipation. ESL students may need more time to decode what is meant by the question and to find the right words and grammar to express themselves (Purdy 2008). Giving questions in advance and/or allowing time to jot down an answer after posing a question in class can support the needs of ESL students.

THE STUDENT ROLE IN QUESTIONING

Questioning is a two-way interaction. Once the instructor is familiar with the range of questions and the expectations, then we turn to the student. There is a significant body of literature that demonstrates students need support to develop and utilize higher-order strategies—including questioning—even at the college and university level. When asked to generate questions themselves, students most often generate fact-level questions (e.g., Dillon 1988; Özerk 2001). Part of the instructor's role then is "teaching" students to be able to ask as well as respond to challenging higher-order questions.

Teaching students how to generate and respond to higher-order questions has many advantages. Students who have this skill can study more effectively because they can ask themselves meaningful questions. Students who know how to ask higher-order questions are more likely to generate these questions for their peers and their instructors, and this will enhance their own learning as well as the learning of others (King 1994).

Within the field of cognitive development, many theoretical and empirical papers identify successful learners as those who engage in self-regulated learning (e.g., Paris and Paris 2001; Pintrich 1995; Zimmerman 1989). In other words, these learners have extensive domain knowledge, are intrinsically motivated to learn, engage in metacognitive behaviors that allow them to monitor their behavior and performance, set goals, use sophisticated strategies, and often coordinate many strategies at once (Perry et al. 2002; Willoughby, Wood, and Khan 1994; Willoughby, Wood, and Kraftcheck 2003). Questioning is one of the effective strategies that self-directed learners use (Pressley 2002). However, higher-order questioning strategies rarely appear spontaneously. They need to be taught, and the best means is through direct, explicit instruction (Wood et al. 1999). Instructors can do this by giving students an opportunity to use higher-order questions in small groups, and/or alone as a study aid (King 1989; Willoughby et al. 2000). Instructors can model use of these questions while teaching and comment on how questions are shaping the discussion as they proceed through their classes. For example, instructors can identify when they are going beyond the information given, when they elaborate, and when they draw on personal knowledge. Instructors can provide students with basic question stems that the students can then fill in relevant endings for topics covered across the class (e.g., "Explain why . . ."; "Why is . . . important?"; How does . . . relate to what we studied earlier?"; see King 1994, 165). By providing students with the practice they need to use questioning strategies effectively, instructors will provide students with an effective learning tool, as well as prepare them for interaction in the classroom.

REFERENCES

Bloom, Benjamin S. 1956. *Taxonomy of educational objectives: The classification of educational goals. Handbook 1*. New York: McKay.

Bloom, Benjamin S., John T. Hastings, and George F. Madaus. 1971. *Handbook on formative and summative evaluation of student learning*. New York: McGraw-Hill.

Cazden, Courtney B. 2001. *Classroom discourse the language of teaching and learning*. 2nd ed. Portsmouth, NH: Heinemann.

Dillon, James T. 1988. *Questioning and teaching: A manual of practice*. New York: Teachers College Press.

Good, Thomas L., Ricky L. Slavings, Kathleen Hobson Harel, and Hugh Emerson. 1987. Student passivity: A study of question asking in K–12 classrooms. *Sociology of Education*, 60(3): 181–199.

Greeson, Larry E. 1988. College classroom interaction as a function of teacher and student-centered instruction. *Teaching and Teacher Education*, 4(4): 305–315.

Karabenick, Stuart A. 1994. Relation of perceived teacher support of student questioning to students' beliefs about teacher attributions for questioning and perceived classroom learning environment. *Learning and Individual Differences*, 6(2): 187–204.

King, Alison. 1989. Effects of self-questioning training on college students' comprehension of lectures. *Contemporary Educational Psychology*, 14(4): 366–381.

King, Alison. 1994. Autonomy and question asking: The role of personal control in guided student-generated questioning. *Learning and Individual Differences*, 6(2): 163–185.

King, Alison. 1995a. Designing the instructional process to enhance critical thinking across the curriculum. *Teaching of Psychology*, 22(1): 13–17.

King, Alison. 1995b. Cognitive strategies for learning from direct instruction. In Eileen Wood, Vera E. Woloshyn, and Teena Willoughby (Eds.), *Cognitive strategy instruction for middle and high schools*. Cambridge, MA: Brookline Books.

McKeachie, Wilbert, and Marilla Svinicki. 2006. *McKeachie's teaching tips: Strategies, research and theory for college and university teachers*. Boston: Houghton-Mifflin.

Myers, Scott A., Chad Edwards, Shawn T. Wahl, and Matthew M. Martin. 2007. The relationship between perceived instructor aggressive communication and college-student involvement. *Communication Education*, 56(4): 495–508.

Özerk, Kamil. 2001. Teacher–student verbal interaction and questioning, class size and bilingual students' academic performance. *Scandinavian Journal of Educational Research*, 45(4): 353–367.

Paris, Scott G., and Alison H. Paris. 2001. Classroom applications of research on self-regulated learning. *Educational Psychologist*, 36(2): 89–102.

Perry, Nancy E., Karen O. Vandekamp, Louise K. Mercer, and Carla J. Nordby. 2002. Investigating teacher–student interactions that foster self-regulated learning. *Educational Psychologist*, 37(1): 5–15.

Pintrich, Paul R. 1995. Understanding self-regulated learning. *New Directions for Teaching and Learning*, 63(Fall): 3–12.

Pressley, Michael. 2002. *Reading instruction that works: The case for balanced teaching*. 2nd ed. New York: Guilford Press.

Purdy, Joyce. 2008. Inviting conversation: Meaningful talk about texts for English language learners. *Literacy*, 42(1): 44–51.

Skidmore, D., Perez-Parent, M. and Arnfield, S. 2003. Teacher–pupil dialogue in the guided reading session. *Reading, Literacy and Language*, 37(2): 47–53.

Weaver, Robert R., and Jiang Qi. 2005. Classroom organization and participation: College students' perceptions. *Journal of Higher Education*, 76(5): 570–601.

Willoughby, Teena, Eileen Wood, and Mustaq Khan. 1994. Isolating variables that impact or detract from the effectiveness of elaboration strategies. *Journal of Educational Psychology*, 86(2): 279–289.

Willoughby, Teena, Eileen Wood, and Erin R. Kraftcheek. 2003. When can a lack of structure facilitate strategic processing of information? *British Journal of Educational Psychology*, 73(1): 59–69.

Willoughby, Teena, Eileen Wood, Catherine McDermott, and Jennifer McLaren. 2000. Enhancing learning through strategy instruction and group interaction: Is active generation of elaborations critical? *Applied Cognitive Psychology*, 14(1): 19–30.

Wisher, Robert A., and Arthur C. Graesser. 2006. Question-asking in advanced distributed learning environments. In Stephen M. Fiore and Eduardo Salas (Eds.), *Toward a science of distributed learning and training* (pp. 209–234). Washington, DC: American Psychological Association.

Wood, Eileen, Teena Willoughby, Catherine McDermott, Mary Motz, Violet Kasper, and Mary Jo DuCharme. 1999. Developmental differences in study behaviour. *Journal of Educational Psychology*, 91(3): 527–536.

Wood, Eileen, Vera E. Woloshyn, and Teena Willoughby. 1999. *Cognitive strategy instruction for middle and high schools*. Cambridge, MA: Brookline Books.

Zimmerman, Barry J. 1989. A social cognitive view of self-regulated academic learning. *Journal of Educational Psychology*, 81(3): 329–339.

Strategies for Engaging Students with Learning Disabilities

Jacqueline A. Specht
University of Western Ontario

> The Information Processing age is making postsecondary
> education a personal and national necessity.
> (Scott, McGuire, and Shaw 2003, 369)

More and more students with disabilities are enrolling in postsecondary education. A current estimate is that six to nine percent of freshmen in a four-year college or university program have a disability. Of these students, about forty percent have learning disabilities. This is perhaps not too surprising given just under fifty percent of students in the elementary and secondary systems are identified as having a learning disability. What is a learning disability? Weber and Bennett (2004) note that, while a universal definition of learning disability has not yet been agreed upon, there is a general consensus that a learning disability involves general difficulty with information, especially that which is language based. In addition, the challenges the individual faces cannot be explained by either an intellectual or a sensory disability.

There is still concern among many professors about the inclusion of students with learning disabilities in postsecondary education. Many feel that these students do not belong in an institute of higher learning. The biggest concern expressed by many professors is maintaining the integrity of education. However, the inclusion of individuals with learning disabilities is not about compromising the curriculum, rather it is about understanding that differential learning should not prevent one from obtaining a postsecondary education. Barring students who have the intellectual ability from the academic world because of a learning disability would be an unnecessarily harsh and shortsighted decision. Postsecondary education is becoming a must in Western society. Students who graduate from college on average earn between fifty-eight and ninety-two percent more than those who do not graduate. The ability to earn money in Western society allows for many more opportunities, both in terms of career and life plans. Knowing this, many students with learning disabilities want to be able to pursue postsecondary education as an option. In response, universities have begun to open their doors to a growing number of individuals representing an array of diverse needs. As a result, we, as professors must be willing to assist these individuals in achieving their goals.

The onus is now on us, as educators, to move forward and take our profession of teaching in directions that are new to the mainstream postsecondary environment. How can we change our teaching practice? If we look at the work of Chickering and Gamson (1987), we see that good teaching practice:

- Encourages contact between students and faculty
- Develops reciprocity and communication among students
- Encourages active learning
- Gives prompt feedback
- Emphasizes active learning
- Communicates high expectations
- Respects diverse talents and ways of learning

Key issues for students with disabilities are that they want to be treated respectfully, they value instructor flexibility, and they require instructor-student confidentiality concerning their learning issues. Good practice as previously outlined allows us to address these concerns. When we provide for student with disabilities, we are providing for all students. Being aware of issues faced by students with disabilities in the class allows us to be aware of the learning needs of all diverse students (e.g., students for whom English is not their first language, students from other cultures, students from impoverished backgrounds). How do we make these changes? We make accommodations.

ACCOMMODATING STUDENTS

When we have students with disabilities in our class, the most typical scenario is that we receive a letter from the center for students with disabilities and we are asked to provide some sort of accommodation based on assessments of the students' learning needs. The most typical types of accommodations come in the form of extended time on tests, tests written in a distraction free area, note takers in class or access to another student's notes, and the use of assistive technology in the class to take notes. Interestingly enough, research has found that faculty report that the most difficult tasks that students with learning disabilities encounter are in class and involve taking notes, completing written assignments during class, and presenting and interpreting ideas orally in class (Ganschow, Philips, and Schneider 2001). Only one area of concern is actually addressed by the accommodations typically provided (i.e., taking notes). Therefore, it seems that we need to do much more than simply allowing an alternate way for students with learning disabilities to obtain notes, we need find ways to engage these students while in class. If they are not engaged, they will not learn. One of the main problems with teaching students with disabilities is that many instructors have little or no formal training in effective strategies for instruction and have not come in contact with people with learning disabilities (Gregg 2007). One way to be ready is to become familiar with the assistance that is available for students on your campus. Ouellett (2004) suggests asking yourself the following questions:

- Are you generally familiar with the services provided by the disability services offices on campus?
- Do you understand the process by which a student is expected to provide you with the documentation of their disability and the appropriate accommodations?
- Do you have the strategies to approach a student with a disability and to engage him or her respectfully about learning goals and needs in the context of this course?

UNIVERSAL DESIGN FOR LEARNING

By using accommodations, such as those listed in the previous section, we are focusing on the shortcomings of the students rather than on those of the program. The Universal Design for Learning (UDL) approach looks more at the program than the student. It was developed by the Center for Applied Special Technology (CAST). According to the CAST, the goal of education is not mastery of knowledge, but rather mastery of learning. The biggest barrier to creating expert learners is the inflexible one-size-fits-all curricula. UDL is based on the architectural concept of "universal design" developed by Ron Mace from North Carolina State University. As society was becoming more aware of accessibility issues for people with physical disabilities and legislation was developed to create physically accessible areas, buildings were designed to be universally accessible. Universal design implies that if buildings were built to accommodate people with disabilities without need for special assistance, everyone would benefit. A common example is that of wheelchair ramps and automatic doors, which became useful for parents with strollers and delivery people with full arms. The phrase "necessary for some, good for all" has been used to describe this movement of universal design.

Scott, McGuire, and Shaw (2003) note that if students in wheelchairs did not need special assistance because the environment was physically accessible, then why could we not create an instructionally accessible environment for the student with learning disabilities? If we create instructionally accessible environments, we could omit the need for special accommodations for just a few people. UDL was promoted by the CAST in the early 1990s primarily for the elementary and secondary school curriculum. The three guiding principles are: provide multiple means of representation, provide multiple means of expression, and provide multiple means of engagement. These principles fit well for students with learning disabilities where the implication is that they have difficulty with one, two, or all of the following: taking in information (representation), integrating the information with what they already know (engagement), or expressing their answers based on what they already know and what they have taken in (expression). Demonstrating to students that there is not one correct way of conveying information makes the curriculum much more accessible. For example, we can present information to students in visual and verbal format. We can assess their learning through essays, tests, posters, plays, and so on. Universal Instructional Design (UID) was a term coined by Silver, Bourke, and Strehorn (1998) for the postsecondary population. Both have the similar goal of enabling students with diverse learning needs to have equal access to the classroom teaching and learning. Given that most students' needs are in the classroom, simply providing extra time on the test does not make the curriculum accessible. UID allows faculty to think about what they teach, why and how they teach, and why and how they assess student learning (Pilner and Johnson 2004). Scott, McGuire, and Shaw (2003) take the principles of universal design and use them in the university setting to provide some useful examples of operating in the classroom. These are not meant to be exhaustive, and they refer to diverse learning needs rather than only learning disabilities to indicate how universal design is good for all.

PRINCIPLE 1— Equitable Use. By providing notes online for students, they can be accessed by all students prior to class to orient them to what will be happening in class. As an advance organizer, they can access their prior knowledge about the information and come to class more prepared. More prepared students are better able to participate in class discussions. Students who have vision loss can read them with enlarged fonts or have them read with a text-to-speech software program. Students with hearing loss can access them visually. Students with a reading disability can take longer to process them or have them read with a text-to-speech program. Students whose first language is not English can take longer to process the information.

PRINCIPLE 2—Flexibility in Use. Instructors who present their material in a variety of ways allow students to access the curriculum in ways that are meaningful to them. Lecturing with an outline, small and large group discussions, and group activities like role playing are just some examples that will engage more learners. Additionally, if there are key terms or discipline-specific jargon that will be used, provide students with this information in advance.

PRINCIPLE 3—Simple and Intuitive. Students should know what is expected of them. There are many ways to achieve this end, but students should not be surprised by their mark on an assignment or in the course. A rubric outlining expectations or a syllabus with detailed information on the assignments are two ways to ensure that students know how to do well in the class. In keeping with Principle 1, electronic copies of these expectations make them accessible for the students. Providing students with one or two questions that they should be able to answer by the end of class allows them to determine if they understand the material.

PRINCIPLE 4—Perceptible Information. Regardless of the students' sensory abilities, they should be able to access the information. In selecting instructional material, it is useful if it is accessible in digital format so that students can access it in traditional hard copy format or digitally should they require assistive technology (like the text-to-speech option in Principle 1) to access the information. In class, speak clearly and at a relaxed pace so that students can process the information presented.

PRINCIPLE 5—Tolerance for Error. By the very nature of differences in learners, we should prepare our courses to allow for different paces and styles of learning in our students. Practice exercises, feedback along the way for student projects, allowing students to drop their lowest mark or substitute marks are all ways to allow for learning to occur. The belief that we must be the ones to weed out students is really not what teaching should be about. Teaching is about opening minds, stimulating interest, and sharing our passion for the areas we study. Additionally, we can teach our students strategies for learning in order to help them be more successful. In one study, Harrison and Beres (2007) noted that poor writers in the university setting tended to focus on mechanical changes in their writing (spelling, grammar, and punctuation), whereas good writers tended to focus on higher-order concepts, such as organization and content. By teaching students to focus on the higher-order issues and strategies for remembering to do that, we can help them minimize some of the errors that they might be making.

PRINCIPLE 6—Low Physical Effort. When physical effort is not part of the curriculum (as it may be in kinesiology courses for example), the nonessential physical effort should be minimized. This can be accomplished by allowing students to use a word processor, have a note taker in class and have help with writing essays and exams.

PRINCIPLE 7—Size and Space for Approach and Use. Regardless of a person's size, posture, mobility, and communication needs, the space needs to be used to the best of your ability. For example, small group discussion works best if people are facing each other. This configuration allows them to see facial expressions as well as hear group members better.

PRINCIPLE 8—A Community of Learners. Communication among students and between students and faculty is encouraged. Study groups, chat rooms, and group work are all ways to encourage communication. In this age of technology, it is perfectly okay to set boundaries. Students often think that e-mail messages should be answered immediately. Faculty are allowed to say that they do (or do not) check e-mail at certain times of the day or on certain days of the week.

PRINCIPLE 9—Instructional Climate. High expectations exist for all students, but instruction is welcome and inclusive. Stating such expectations up front may be necessary in order for students to understand that disrespectful behavior will not be tolerated. The university classroom should be a place for good discussion, often with opposing views. However, we must be respectful in our discussion. Diversity is to be valued by all. Faculty need to specify and model the kinds of exchanges and expectations that will permit a "safe" and respectful learning environment (both in the classroom and online).

CONCLUSION

By understanding the nine principles of universal design as they apply to the classroom we can become more understanding of students with disabilities and therefore more engaging in the classroom. As students feel engaged, they will make efforts to participate in classroom discussion.

See the "For Further Reflection and Action" section at the end of the book for more ideas on adapting your class to accommodate students with learning disabilities.

REFERENCES

Chickering, Arthur W., and Zelda F. Gamson. 1987. Seven principles for good practice in undergraduate education. *American Association of Higher Education Bulletin*, *39*(7): 3–7.

Ganschow, Leonore, Lois Philips, and Elke Schneider. 2001. Closing the gap: Accommodating students with language learning disabilities in college. *Topics in Language Disorders*, *21*(2): 17–37.

Gregg, Noel. 2007. Underserved and unprepared: Postsecondary learning disabilities. *Learning Disabilities Research & Practice*, *22*(4): 219–228.

Harrison, Gina L., and Deborah Beres. 2007. The writing strategies of post-secondary students with writing difficulties. *Exceptionality Education Canada*, *17*(2): 221–242.

Ouellett, Matthew. 2004. Faculty development and the universal instructional design. *Equity & Excellence*, *37*(2): 135–144.

Pilner, Susan M., and Julia R. Johnson. 2004. Historical, theoretical, and foundational principles of universal instructional design in higher education. *Equity and Excellence in Education*, *37*(2): 105–113.

Scott, Sally S., Joan M. McGuire, and Stan F. Shaw. 2003. Universal design for instruction: A new paradigm for adult instruction in postsecondary education. *Remedial and Special Education*. Special issue: Adults with Learning Disabilities, *24*(6): 369–379.

Silver, Patricia, Andrew Bourke, and K. C. Strehorn. 1998. Universal instructional design in higher education: An approach for inclusion. *Equity & Excellence in Education*, *31*(2): 47–51.

Weber, Ken, and Sheila Bennett. 2004. *Special education in Ontario schools*. 5th ed. Niagara-on-the-Lake, Ontario, Canada: Highland Press.

Mind Mapping

Engaging Students

Ernest Biktimirov
Brock University

INTRODUCTION

Having a stimulating classroom discussion is a challenge, even for experienced instructors. Students' different backgrounds, motivations, and learning styles create numerous teaching barriers. In addition, some students struggle to follow discussion, while others are simply reluctant to speak up. To address these challenges, instructors need to use all available teaching tools to engage students, highlight the main points and their interrelations, and provide structure for the discussion.

In this article, I recommend a unique and powerful tool—mind mapping—a technique for developing a visual, nonlinear representation of ideas and their relationships. With colors, images, and key words, mind mapping stimulates both sides of the human brain and enhances its learning potential. As an introduction to mind mapping, Figure 1 features a mind map that visually summarizes the organization and content of the material presented.

MIND MAPPING

Tony Buzan (1991) developed mind mapping based on research about the human brain and psychology of learning. As a result, the process of drawing a mind map resembles how the human brain processes and stores new information. A main idea is depicted in a central image with related ideas radiating in all different directions as branches. To engage the right side of our brain, which is responsible for visual thinking, each branch is high-

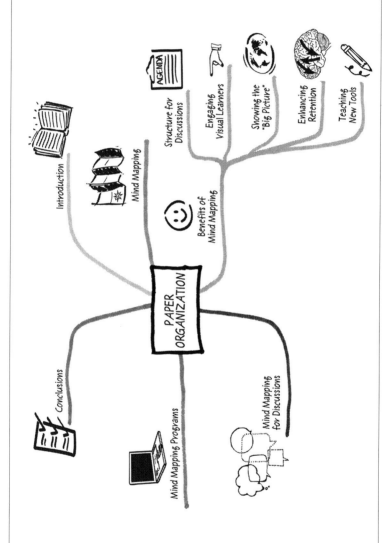

Figure 1. Mind map of the organization of the paper

lighted with its own color (represented by shades of grey here) and an associated key image or word. Supporting concepts radiate as thinner branches from the higher-level branches. Arrows show the variety of relationships among different topics. Originally developed for effective note taking, mind mapping has been adopted for a variety of applications, including writing papers, public speaking, and creative thinking.

Benefits of Mind Mapping

Mind mapping can offer several benefits for generating thought-provoking discussions. First, the process of building a mind map closely follows the main steps of a typical classroom discussion. At the beginning the main idea is identified, then all related secondary topics are developed, and finally relationships among all the topics are established. As a result, mind maps facilitate well-structured discussions.

Second, mind maps use their colors, images, and symbols to engage the more visual learners who are frequently neglected in a traditional classroom discussion. In addition, the process of drawing a mind map during a discussion provides a useful visual reference for students. This reference helps students follow the discussion, see how it progresses, and contribute to it.

Third, mind maps enable students to see the "big picture" of the discussed material. They show the importance of different topics and the variety of relations among them.

Fourth, mind maps facilitate the retention of the discussed material. As a matter of fact, well-constructed mind maps are almost impossible to forget. Moreover, mind maps provide a tangible result of the discussion that can serve as a useful reference for future studies.

Finally, by using mind mapping, instructors introduce students to a tool that will benefit them not only in their studies, but also in future careers. Mind mapping has a wide range of applications, such as problem solving, project management, and public presentations. In fact, mind mapping "can be used in nearly every activity where thought, recall, planning or creativity are involved" (Buzan 1991, 107).

Using Mind Mapping for Discussions

Mind mapping can be used for generating stimulating classroom discussions in a number of ways. Two strategies are presented next as examples. In the first strategy, an instructor leads the discussion and draws a mind map as the discussion progresses, while in the second strategy students

33

use mind maps to facilitate discussions in their small groups, and then present the prepared mind maps to the whole class.

To illustrate the first strategy, mind mapping is described to review capital budgeting techniques in an introductory finance course (Biktimirov and Nilson 2006). Capital budgeting techniques are an important topic in introductory corporate finance, and it frequently creates difficulty for students because of the large number of discussed techniques. As a rule, at least six different capital budgeting techniques are covered, and by the end of the lecture students often feel overwhelmed and struggle with understanding the relationships among the techniques. I have found that a discussion accompanied by drawing a mind map at the end of the lecture reinforces the main points and helps students see "the big picture" by placing all the pieces together.

A mind map provides a useful structure for academic discussion. The development of a mind map begins with the main idea in the center of the page, just like a typical discussion usually starts with the question: "What is the main idea of the topic?" I ask students what the main purpose of capital budgeting is and why we need to know capital budgeting techniques. Then, through discussion, we conclude that we need capital budgeting techniques to differentiate between profitable projects and unprofitable ones. In other words, capital budgeting techniques serve as a financial crystal ball to help us predict the future outcomes of projects. Therefore, we start our mind map with an image of a crystal ball with a dollar sign in the center of the page (Figure 2). As I start drawing a mind map on the board, I recommend the students follow me by making mind maps in their notes.

I then ask the students to identify the crucial difference between all these techniques. Through discussion with the students we conclude that the main difference is that some techniques ignore the time value of money, while others take it into account. To reinforce this important point, we draw two branches that grow from the central image in opposite directions. We use different colors (shown here with shading) for each branch and clearly separate them on the mind map. The branch that ignores the time value of money is shown in the bottom left part of the mind map, whereas the branch that takes into account the time value of money is in the top right. The higher positioning of the latter branch emphasizes the fact that considering the time value of money results in more advanced techniques.

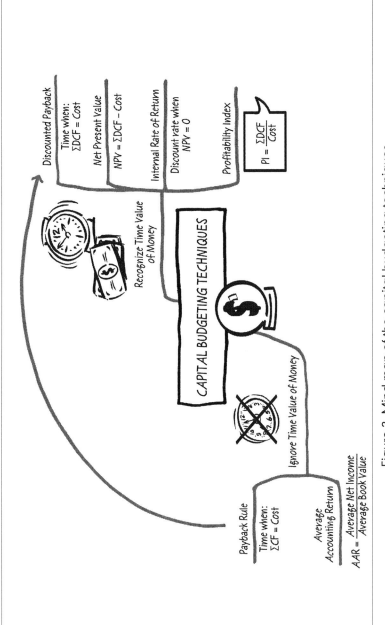

Figure 2. Mind map of the capital budgeting techniques

To engage all students and to make the mind map memorable, relevant images for each important concept are added. For example, a crossed-out clock illustrates the branch that ignores the time value of money. To suggest the time value connection for the other branch, the image of the clock connected to a dollar bill is used. At this stage, the mind map appearing on the board provides a visual reference for the students and helps them follow the discussion and contribute to it.

Next we develop each branch further through discussion. We identify two techniques that ignore the time value of money and four techniques that take it into account. Then we recall how each technique is calculated and put concise formulas next to each technique.

There is no limit to how many levels each branch can have. For this topic, another layer is warranted that highlights the advantages and disadvantages of each method and could be added. Given the large number of techniques, understanding their strong and weak features will help students to choose the most appropriate technique for specific problems later in the course. Again, the use of visuals is important for understanding and retaining the material. For example, we associate a smiling face to mark advantages and a sad face to mark disadvantages.

At this stage, the developed mind map allows students to see "the big picture" and understand how different techniques are related. For example, an arrow going from Payback Rule to Discounted Payback reinforces that Discounted Payback is an extension of Payback Rule by taking the time value of money into account.

The developed mind map serves as a tangible result of the discussion and a useful reference tool for exam preparation. As a matter of fact, once they have been drawn, mind maps are almost impossible to forget.

One problem with conducting discussions in large classes is giving each student an opportunity to contribute. This problem becomes more pronounced given the fact that some students are reluctant to speak up in front of a large group of their peers. In such situations, instructors can use the second strategy for using mind maps for discussion.

In this strategy, the instructor divides the class into small groups and asks them to discuss a topic. Based on these discussions, each group produces a mind map on flip chart paper or a transparency for presentation to the class. During these presentations, other students are encouraged to ask questions and any member of the presenting group can respond. This setting creates a discussion environment in which students play a more active role. After several groups have had a chance to present their mind maps, the instructor can summarize and review the main points by drawing a final mind map on the board.

This strategy, which uses small groups, makes it easier for students to participate in the discussion, especially for those who are hesitant to share their opinions in front of the whole class. It also limits the negative effect of vocal students who can dominate classroom discussion.

I have received positive feedback on the use of mind maps from my students. They often mentioned that mind maps helped them understand the topic, especially the relationships between different concepts. They also appreciated having a mind map as a tangible result of the discussion that could be used for future reference. Moreover, some students mentioned they continued using the technique in other courses.

Colleagues have also liked the idea of using mind mapping for teaching. At the request of my colleagues, I have been conducting annual workshops for both undergraduate and graduate students for the last ten years. I have also facilitated mind mapping workshops for instructors from different disciplines in Canada and the United States. After each workshop, participants expressed their enthusiasm for this tool and shared plans for integrating it into their teaching.

Mind Mapping Programs

While mind maps can be drawn manually on a blackboard, whiteboard, or overhead transparency, they also can be created on a computer using mind mapping programs. Computer-generated mind maps offer a number of advantages: they can be easily shared, stored, or shown on the Internet with incorporated hyperlinks; they can include audio and video files; and they can be easily exported into different programs, such as Microsoft Word and PowerPoint. Table 1 summarizes basic information on available mind mapping programs.

All programs can be downloaded and examined for free during a trial period. In addition, companies give educational discounts or offer lower-priced versions (MindGenius Education V2 and Visual Mind 9.1 Basic Edition). Inspiration Software develops its products specifically for educators and has the lowest prices. Some of the companies also offer quantity discounts and network licensing to accommodate course and schoolwide installations.

All programs work with the Windows operating systems, while ConceptDraw, Inspiration, and MindManager have Macintosh versions as

PRODUCT	PRICE/ EDUCATIONAL DISCOUNT	OPERATING SYSTEMS	OTHER VERSIONS	COMPANY INFORMATION	
				Name	Telephone/internet
ConceptDraw MINDMAP 5 Personal	$119/Yes	Windows; Macintosh	Professional	Computer Systems Odessa, Ltd.	1 (877) 441-1150 www.conceptdraw.com
Inspiration 8	$69/No	Windows; Macintosh; Palm OS; Pocket PC	Kidspiration 3	Inspiration Software, Inc.	1-800-877-4292 www.inspiration.com
MindGenius Education V2	$114/No	Windows	Business V2; Home V2	MindGenius Ltd.	+44 (0) 1355-247766 www.mindgenius.com
MindManager Pro 7	$349/Yes	Windows; Macintosh	Lite 7	Mindjet	1-877-646-3538 www.mindjet.com
MindMapper 2008 Standard	$124.95/Yes	Windows	Professional; Junior	SimTech Systems, Inc.	1-940-455-2671 www.mindmapper.com
VisiMap Professional 4.1	$143/Yes	Windows	Not available	CoCo Systems Ltd.	+44 7971-321586 www.visimap.com
Visual Mind 9.1 Basic Edition	$109/No	Windows	Business Edition	Mind Technologies AS	+47 3285 5455 www.visual-mind.com

Table 1. Summary of basic information on available mind mapping programs

well. In addition, Inspiration can be used on handheld devices (Palm OS and Pocket PC).

All programs listed in Table 1 are easy to learn and use. They usually come with tutorials, templates, sample mind maps, and large libraries of images and symbols. In addition, users can choose from a large selection of colors, shapes, and fonts to emphasize different ideas. For the latest information on available programs, visit the companies' web sites.

CONCLUSION

Mind mapping facilitates classroom discussion in a number of ways by offering structure, engaging visual learners, showing the "big picture," promoting retention, and teaching new tools. In addition, mind mapping is easy and fun. The visual nature of mind mapping makes it a unique and effective teaching tool in any instructor's toolbox. To be more proficient at the craft of teaching, we should use all of the tools at our disposal.

BIBLIOGRAPHY

Biktimirov, Ernest N., and Linda B. Nilson. 2006. Show them the money: Using mind mapping in the introductory finance course. *Journal of Financial Education*, 32(Fall): 72–86.

Buzan, Tony. 1991. *Use both sides of your brain*. 3rd ed. New York: Plume.

Buzan, Tony, and Barry Buzan. 1996. *The mind map book: How to use radiant thinking to maximize your brain's untapped potential*. New York: Plume.

Eriksson, Larse T., and Amie M. Hauer. 2004. Mind map marketing: A creative approach in developing marketing skills. *Journal of Marketing Education*, 26(2): 174–187.

Farrand, Paul, Fearzana Hussain, and Enid Hennessy. 2002. The efficacy of the "mind map" study technique. *Medical Education*, 36(May): 426–431.

Margulies, Nancy, and Nusa Maal. 2002. *Mapping inner space: Learning and teaching visual mapping*. 2nd ed. Tucson, AZ: Zephyr Press.

Mento, Anthony J., Patrick Martinelli, and Raymond M. Jones. 1999. Mind mapping in executive education: Applications and outcomes. *The Journal of Management Development*, 18(4): 390–407.

Wycoff, Joyce. 1991. *Mindmapping: Your personal guide to exploring creativity and problem-solving*. New York: Berkley Publishing Group.

Part Two

Engaging Students in a Variety of Settings

The Dreaded Pause

Initiating and Sustaining Discussion in a Small- to Medium-Sized Classroom

Kathy Cawsey
Dalhousie University

We all know the moment: standing in front of a classroom, looking out at a spread of expectant faces, asking the question. And then … there's the pause. And we wait. And the students wait. Our stomachs start churning in anxiety. The sweat breaks out on the back of our necks. The students start squirming. The question hangs. Along with it hangs the unspoken question: will a good discussion get started, or will we revert back to safe, comfortable, boring lecture mode?

Many articles on the subject of discussion-based classroom learning begin with the questions: the kinds of questions, the methods of questioning, and the purposes of asking different kinds of questions (Barnes 1983; Bateman 1990; Chalmers and Fuller 1996, 81–82; Davis 1993, 66–69; Jacobson 1984; Kasulis 1984; Miller and Miller 1997, 132–136; refer also to Wood, in Part One, above). It is my belief that while many people focus a great deal of energy in generating important and stimulating questions, they also need to consider what happens after the question is delivered. The pause is an equally important part of the discussion.

Great questions are important, of course, but an instructor can have a list of fantastic questions twenty pages long and yet never get a good discussion going. The pause after the question matters: Handle it well, and you have laid the groundwork for a full term of solid, enlightening, pedagogically challenging discussions. Handle it poorly, and you may as well skip straight to January—you'll be lecturing for the rest of this term (Tiberius 1995, chap. 5).

The pause is a tricky thing. If it is too short, students learn that you will answer your own questions, and you will never get a discussion started. If it is too long, the students will become uncomfortable and resentful, and you will never get a discussion started. This article will focus on getting the pause to the Goldilocks level—just right—and the ways that using the pause skillfully can lead to productive, cooperative, intellectually stimulating discussion in the university or college classroom.

DISCUSSION-BASED LEARNING

Many studies have demonstrated the advantages of discussion-based learning, so I will do no more than briefly touch on its merits here (Davis 1993, 63; Timpson and Bendel-Simso 1996, 77). Lectures have their uses, especially when it comes to conveying large amounts of factual information; however, for many pedagogical purposes, discussions are a superior method of teaching and learning. First, students remember better when they are required to actively engage with the subject material and respond to it, rather than passively absorbing information from the professor. Instead of simply learning how to remember and regurgitate, in discussions students are required to explore, synthesize, evaluate, expand on, and process both arguments and information, developing higher-level cognitive skills of critical thinking and analysis (McKeachie 1969, 37; Timpson and Bendel-Simso 1996, 80). These skills are practiced even if particular students do not actively participate in the discussion themselves, because they are needed to understand other students' responses and comments.

Beyond being pedagogically superior to lecturing, discussion-based learning has other advantages. Students not only learn the skills of critical thinking, analysis, and evaluation, they also learn the more extroverted skills of talking in a large group, presenting themselves appropriately in a semiformal situation, formulating their thoughts, communicating those thoughts efficiently and effectively, disagreeing without giving offense, and possibly moderating group discussions themselves. All of these skills will be valuable in arenas far beyond the classroom and will be remembered and used when the "content" of the course is forgotten.

In discussion-based classes, there is a tighter feedback loop than in lecture classes. In traditional classes, the instructor only receives feedback on the effectiveness of her teaching through assignments and tests—and if the midterm is the first graded assessment, then half a term will have passed before the instructor finds out if the students are learning anything. Likewise, students must wait until they receive their midterm grades before they know whether they understand the material properly. By that time, so many subsequent misunderstandings might have accumulated as the result of an initial mistake that the student could be helplessly lost. Moreover, a grade is a poor source of information: the student cannot tell what specifically she does not understand, what the correct interpretation might be, or how she might improve her learning techniques.

In discussion-based courses, by contrast, the feedback loop is almost instantaneous. The instructor should be able to judge from student responses whether they have understood the material; more importantly, he can focus on areas they had difficulty understanding and modify his teaching accordingly. Students can be active in this process by asking questions or arguing points in order to refine their understanding. Also, the students receive immediate feedback as the instructor refines, disagrees with, or expands on their answers. Mistakes are more likely to be corrected quickly so that subsequent learning can build on a solid foundation of understanding. The pedagogical advantages of a tighter feedback loop are obvious.

Discussion-based learning is appealing from an ideological standpoint as well. It is more democratic: students can take more control of the class and make more decisions about the learning process. (It is important to note that these classes are not *fully* democratic: the professor should never completely lose control, and the students don't get to vote on their grades at the end!) Discussion-based classrooms move away from a hierarchical model of learning to one based more on cooperation and collaboration. The communication vectors, rather than being one-way and top-down from professor to student, are two-way or even three-way: from professor to student, from student to professor, and from student to other students. Students tend to enjoy this type of learning more and are more likely to take charge of their own education, rather than deferring the responsibility to the professor.

USING THE PAUSE

Most of us agree on the value of discussion—the problem arises when we try to use it in classrooms. It can be intimidating because it feels as though we are relinquishing control; it also often leads us away from our comfort zone of factual knowledge and expertise; and there is the ever-present worry that no one will talk. As previously discussed, relinquishing control and moving away from our comfort zone may actually be good things —when students take charge of the learning process, both professors and students collaborate in the development of understanding, rather than the professor being the sole authority and repository of knowledge. To conquer the third intimidating aspect of discussion—the prospect of echoing silence—the solution is to *use* the silence, to see it as a tool rather than a threat.

Several techniques can help you use the pause effectively and overcome the threat of silence.

Rhythm

The timing of the pause is its most crucial aspect, and there is a rhythm to it. You ask, you wait, you rephrase, you wait, you narrow down, you wait, you explain.

The waits are crucial. This is the chance for students to think about the question, to formulate their response, to see if anyone else will answer, and to test you to see if they can get away with not answering—if you will answer your own questions. The students are thinking about lots of things, while you are thinking about only one thing: whether anyone will answer the question. As a result, *the pause always feels longer to you than it does to the students.* Wait well past the point of your own discomfort (Davis 1993, 86; Miller and Miller 1997, 137).

However, you do not want the pause to drag on too long or everyone will stop enjoying the class. Nobody likes uncomfortable silence. Therefore, if the silence stretches, you can break it by rephrasing the question—and then wait again. If no one answers at this point, then narrow down the question to make it easier to answer. At no point in this process do you answer the question yourself: each rephrasing or narrowing down of the question should move the class closer to the answer you are aiming for.

In most cases, the professor should start with a fairly broad question—sometimes even too broad. This has several advantages: it allows for answers that you didn't expect; it gives slower-thinking students time to work out their response as you narrow down the question; and it challenges the students by refusing to spoon-feed them. "Leading" questions can be used at times; they are especially good if the students do not understand and you want to take them through the problem-solving process rather than just giving them the answer. However, professors should try not to use leading questions all the time or they will not fully realize the creative potential of discussions; "leading" question-and-answer discussions are really just a lecture in another form.

Sometimes, to avoid the problem of the pause, it is good to start with narrow, easy questions to build the rhythm of question-and-answer and get students comfortable answering. If no one answers this type of question, especially later in the term, it is usually because it's too easy—in that case, ask the class if the question is too easy, answer it yourself, and move on.

The first pause of the term will generally be the longest. As the term goes on, students will learn that you are not going to answer your own questions, and as they themselves become more comfortable with the group dynamics the pauses will get shorter.

Atmosphere

These group dynamics are important in using the pause effectively. The way you use the pause in the first few classes will establish the atmosphere of the class for most of the term; and the atmosphere, in turn, will affect the way in which the students perceive the pause.

You want to establish an atmosphere that is comfortable and trusting, where students feel safe taking risks and being wrong. Some of this comes from the way you respond to the first answers they risk sharing, of course, and I discuss this in the section "After the Pause" at the end of this article. But much of the atmosphere is established through your own body language, manner, and expectations as you wait through the first couple of pauses of the term.

The atmosphere during the pause should be expectant but not pressured. You expect the students to answer, but you are not guilt-tripping or threatening them into answering; *not answering must always be an option*. Nonetheless, you should convey expectancy and anticipation through your facial expressions and body language: look around the class, be attentive to the mood, and catch people's eyes (Davis 1993, 69). Avoid looking stressed or nervous about the silence—perch on the desk, stick your hands in your pockets, and lean back as though you have all the time in the world to wait for the students to answer.

Once you overcome your own anxiety about silence and stop listening to your inner voices about how long the silence has lasted, the atmosphere of the classroom will tell you how long to pause. If students are looking at you, checking around the class to see who will answer, or gazing upward, they are thinking or gathering the courage to answer; give them more time. Raise your eyebrows or nod at a student who looks as though she has the answer, or—especially once the class is well established—call on her by name and say "you look as though you have an idea." (Yes, you should know the name of every student in your class, even in classes as large as 100 students. This seems overwhelming, but *nothing* has more impact on the atmosphere of the class or the respect the students will have for you. I bring a digital camera to the first few classes and ask the students to pose for mug shots holding signs with their names; they hate it, but it means I can have all their names memorized within a week.)

If, instead of keeping their heads up during the pause, the students tuck their heads down, avoid eye contact, or look confused, annoyed, or bored, don't let the pause stretch (Davis 1993, 71). They either do not know the answer or are refusing to answer for some other reason. This is the moment where you need to change tack.[1]

Alternatives to the Pause

The third technique for making the pause work for you is to change tack slightly—to fill the silence without answering the question. This technique is different from rephrasing or narrowing down the question; instead it is a tool used to make the class more comfortable or to change the atmosphere. In this case you temporarily release the class from the obligation of answering, returning to the question only when the class is emotionally more able to answer it.

One way to do this is to crack a joke or tell an anecdote. The joke or story must be relevant to the topic at hand, of course, and should arise out of it. The humor can pick up on the class's negative, "forbidden" feelings about the subject: a joke about the long-windedness of the author, for example, or an ironic crack about the "tolerance and understanding" of the Spanish Inquisition will show the students that you understand their initial negative reaction, but that you want them to move past that to a more rounded understanding of the subject. An anecdote about your own difficulties as a student when facing the same subject will put you "all on the same side" and let the students know that it is alright to feel confused or to make mistakes.

Another option is to ask the class if they understand the question or if you need to go back and explain something better. This is tricky because if you sound patronizing or impatient, the class will clam up even tighter than before. You need to convey the sense that you truly want to find out if they understand, and that you perceive any problems in understanding to be your problem because you haven't been clear enough, and not theirs. If a whole class looks apathetic, one thing that often works is to ask a simple question (such as "do you understand?" or "am I going too fast?"), and when you receive no response, nod and shake your head exaggeratedly, drawling, "this means yes, this means no." Students are released from the burden of answering—they can simply shake or nod their heads in response to your question—and it usually gets a laugh as well.

Formal Reinforcement

A final aid in shortening the pause is formal reinforcement. Put your grades where your mouth is: if discussion is important to you and to the students' learning, then reward them for it. Give high participation grades. Develop a clear system for evaluating those grades so that you avoid bias (however latent) and can defend the grades you give if need be. I quickly check off every student who participated when I return to my office after class, giving two checks if the participation was particularly insightful or helpful. At the end of term, I divide the number of checks by the number of classes. Make it clear on the syllabus that you value participation, and that participation is an expected part of the class.

Formal reinforcement will never create good discussion if the atmosphere of the class is inhibiting or if you handle the pause poorly. However, it does make your priorities clear and rewards those students who take responsibility for making the discussion work well.

AFTER THE PAUSE

If you handle the pause correctly, it will get shorter and shorter as the term goes on, as students both become more comfortable and learn that you are not going to answer your own questions. The goal of the pause is to get students to answer the question—but how you handle the answer is almost as important as how you handle the pause in ensuring a good discussion will ensue.

Your role, as professor and discussion leader, is multifaceted and includes at least the following activities.

Guiding Discussion

Despite the fact that discussion classes feel more out-of-control than lectures, you should be in control at all times. This does not necessarily mean the discussion should follow a set plan; the joy of the discussion method is that students can raise points that you had not previously thought of and can steer the discussion toward their own interests and challenges. But you should make sure that the discussion remains productive and challenging, and contributes to the learning of the class.

This can be done in a variety of ways: by following up on a student's point with an explanation or detail the students would not know; by asking a follow-up question to push the students' thinking further; by asking students to compare the point just raised to an earlier subject of discussion; and so on. If the discussion is becoming unproductive, say so (often this is best done with humor: "Okay, okay, okay, we're waaay off base—let's get back to the differences between communism and capitalism … ."). If the discussion is getting too chaotic, feel free to delay some points either by writing them on the board to return to later or by asking a student to "hold that thought." It is important to remember and return to those comments, even if only to acknowledge that you didn't have time to return to them: "We've only got two minutes and we haven't managed to talk about Yin's comment about socialism—hmmm, that might make a good exam question!"

Sometimes you will get a comment that I call a "left-field" comment —one that seems entirely unrelated to the subject at hand. Rather than just ignoring the comment, ask the student how her point relates to the discussion and ask her to substantiate her claim: "Interesting, Marcy. Where are you seeing this in the text?" This teaches the student to justify and make explicit her reasoning, and soon she will begin to incorporate such explanation into her future comments.

Refereeing Discussion

Part of guiding the discussion is, of course, juggling the responses of several people at once. It can feel overwhelming when twenty hands go up at once, but remember, this is a good thing—the students are interested and involved. Always call first on the people who talk the least; the extraverts who always have their hand in the air will understand, and you can wink or nod at them to let them know you find their constant participation valuable. Sometimes it is useful to list students in the turn they will talk: this lets them know you have seen them and allows them to rest their arms. If the discussion becomes heated and people jump in without waiting to be called on, gently remind them to wait their turn.

It is also your job to bring some sort of order to the various comments that are raised—often it is hard for the students to know what comments are most important and which to write down. Repeating or rephrasing students' comments can help do this because you can emphasize points, state them more concisely, and show how they relate to previous points of discussion (this also helps in a large classroom because those at the back will not always be able to hear all the comments). Sorting the comments on the board and grouping them according to subject or theme is another way of prioritizing and schematizing the information and arguments. It is also a good idea to pause and summarize what has been said.

Dealing with Wrong Answers

Dealing with wrong answers is one of the trickiest aspects of discussion-based learning and one of the most crucial in establishing an atmosphere of trust. Don't be afraid to say that a particular answer is wrong—the rest of the class, and the student himself, need to know this. At the same time, you need to reinforce the fact that you appreciate the risk the student has taken and encourage him to answer again. A sympathetic smile and a positive comment can do this: "Good guess, Tom, but I'm afraid not" or "I can see why you might come to that conclusion, but I'm not sure that fits in with . . ."

Another way to deal with wrong answers is to lead the student through the thinking process to let her find where she went wrong. Again, it is crucial that this not be done in a patronizing manner; rather, you are asking the student to justify her conclusion to you. At times, you may find her answer more "correct" than you had initially thought—it may turn out she can indeed justify her argument—or you can praise her correct thinking while allowing her to revise her conclusion. A skillful discussion leader can pick up on a key point in an answer, ignoring the rest, and rephrase it so the class understands where the emphasis should lie.

The most important part of making students feel comfortable with risking wrong answers is admitting when you yourself are wrong. Work out your conclusions aloud, and let them see the process by which you come to an answer—including the wrong ways or dead ends you might take. Keep a list of questions to which you don't know the answer, and check on facts that you are unsure of. Make sure you report back with the correct answer during the following class. And always fully and unreservedly admit when you are wrong (Bateman 1990, 4).

Dealing with Controversy

Part of making students feel comfortable in a discussion is making the classroom a safe place, where they won't be targeted or put down for holding a particular opinion or expressing a particular viewpoint. University classrooms should be places where civilized disagreement is encouraged and welcomed.

The best way to deal with controversy is to establish ground rules from the start. In the syllabus and in the first few classes, establish what behaviors are unacceptable—racist, sexist, or homophobic slurs, for example, or any kind of personal attack or put-down. Have the class agree to a code of behavior. Emphasize that what goes on in the classroom should stay in the classroom: no stupid comments are allowed to be posted on Facebook or "Overheard at . . ." sites, for example. Model the kind of respectful behavior you want them to emulate.

Second, actively encourage controversy so that students become used to disagreeing with one another and defending their position without feeling under attack. After a comment, ask, "Does anyone disagree?" or "What arguments might be used to counter that point?" Encourage students to disagree with your own conclusions and praise them when they do it well. Outline for them the disagreements among scholars in the field you are studying and make it clear that academics themselves rarely agree on everything.

When controversy does arise, make sure the tone of the discussion remains civil and respectful. Deal with unacceptable behavior or language immediately and firmly: "Jason, I am uncomfortable with what you just said because it sounded pretty racist to me. Can you rephrase your comment in a way that won't offend people?" If students are getting upset or emotionally involved, try to shift the ground of the discussion back to the academic side of things: "Whether or not we agree with abortion isn't really at issue here—we could argue all day about this. What I want to talk about is what the character's views on abortion are in the novel and how that affects the story." After class, individually check in with the students most involved in the discussion to make sure they didn't feel too uncomfortable, and in the following class, "debrief" with the class as a whole.

At times, humor and teasing can be used (extremely carefully!) to defuse an emotional discussion. You must get to know each individual student well, and carefully evaluate what level of teasing each student can handle. But often there will be a student who is deliberately stirring up controversy, and these students rarely mind if you point it out: "Okay, so Riley is mostly causing trouble and rabble-rousing here, but she does have a good point about the way 9/11 is seen by other countries ..." In all such cases, a safe atmosphere must be thoroughly established before you can use techniques such as teasing or deliberately stirring up controversy.

Pause Complicators

Two classroom personalities will disturb your skillful handling of the pause-and-answer rhythm: the extreme extrovert and the introvert.

The Extreme Extrovert. This student is relatively rare, but most classes have at least one. The extreme extrovert will not allow a pause to take its course, but will jump in with an answer as soon as you ask the question. Just as students quickly learn that you will answer your own questions, they learn that this particular student will always have an answer, and so they do not have to formulate their own. Moreover, a certain breed of extreme extrovert will go on at length about a topic irrelevant to the discussion, and it will be hard to pull the discussion back to the issue at hand.

Like most issues, if you deal with the extreme extrovert early in the term, the issue will disappear. First, insist on students' raising their hands, rather than just jumping in. After the first couple of questions that she answers, ignore the extreme extrovert's hand until the pause has run its course, so that other students get the chance to think about their answers. You can make this process explicit, saying something like, "Okay folks, Juan's doing all the work here—what do other people think?" In particularly extreme cases, casually mention to the student after class or in office hours that not everyone thinks as quickly as he does, and that you don't always call on him because you're giving other students the chance to think and respond. Suggest that he save his answers for the toughest questions, leaving the easier questions to the other students.

The Introvert. Discussion classes are, by their very nature, unfair to introverts. This does not mean we should drop the use of discussion; on the contrary, introverts have the most to learn from discussion classes. The skills they develop (talking in front of people, expressing their opinions, and overcoming shyness) are crucial skills they will need in almost every workplace. Therefore, it is important that instructors provide structures whereby introverts can contribute to the class and can gradually become more comfortable speaking out loud.

One way to do this is to have online class discussion boards, where introverts can express their opinions outside of class and behind the comforting mask of a computer screen. If you then refer to the online discussion during class time, the students' confidence will be boosted and they may feel more comfortable talking in class. Another method is to have students prepare written "responses" to the discussion: we sometimes forget that listeners are as important to discussions as talkers are, and the introverts are contributing by being attentive listeners. Response papers allow you to give marks for such attentive involvement; moreover, you can use some of the best responses in the following class, in a way that will again build the introverts' confidence in their own ideas.

If you want to encourage introverts to talk in class, not just respond in writing, then a good idea is to provide them with the questions beforehand to give them a chance to think about and develop a response. Then students come to class with answers prepared so they can jump into the discussion without panic. Alternatively, have them pair off for a couple of minutes to discuss the question, then report back to the class (Timpson and Bendel-Simso 1996, 67). In smaller classes, you can go around the circle and ask everyone to respond—the fact that everyone has to do it makes it less scary than cold-calling, and you can start with a couple of extroverts to give the introverts time to think about their answers. Most importantly, make sure that the introverts know their contributions are valuable—and *never* miss their hands if they go up in class.

PAUSING YOURSELF

The final way to encourage the valuable use of the pause is to pause yourself. Encourage the class to ask questions (Don't just say, "Are there any questions?" in a formulaic way, but ask, "What questions do you have?"), and then think before answering their questions (Davis 1993, chap. 11). Show the students that you are taking the time to answer their questions, and that silence is, if not golden, then at least comfortable.

NOTE

1. In electronic classrooms, body language cues are unavailable, and this adds an extra challenge to dealing with the pause. See Cawsey and Lancashire (2009) for discussion on this topic.

REFERENCES

Barnes, Carol P. 1983. Questioning in college classrooms. In Carolyn L. Ellner et al. (Eds.), *Studies of college teaching* (pp. 61–82). Lexington, MA: Lexington Books.

Bateman, Walter. 1990. *Open to question*. San Francisco: Jossey-Bass.

Cawsey, Kathy, and Ian Lancashire. 2009. An online poetry course (for Carol). In Ian Lancashire (Ed.), *Teaching literature and language online* (pp. 310–330). New York: Modern Language Association.

Chalmers, Denise, and Richard Fuller. 1996. *Teaching for learning at university*. London: Kogan Page.

Davis, Barbara Gross. 1993. *Tools for teaching*. San Francisco: Jossey-Bass.

Jacobson, Robert L. 1984. Asking questions is the key skill needed for "discussion teaching." *Chronicle of Higher Education*, July 25: 20.

Kasulis, Thomas. 1984. Questioning. In Margaret Morganroth Gullette (Ed.), *The art and craft of teaching* (pp. 38–48). Cambridge, MA: Harvard University Press.

McKeachie, Wilbert. 1969. *Teaching tips*. Lexington, MA: D.C. Heath.

Miller W. R., and Marie Miller. 1997. *Handbook for college teaching*. Sautee-Nacoochee, GA: PineCrest Publications.

Tiberius, Richard. 1995. *Small group teaching: A trouble-shooting guide*. Toronto, Canada: OISE Press.

Timpson, William, and Paul Bendel-Simso. 1996. *Concepts and choices for teaching*. Madison, WI: Atwood Publishing.

Teaching Large Classes

Mike Atkinson

University of Western Ontario

Whenever I tell people that I teach classes with enrollments of 800 to 1,200, one question always comes to the forefront—why would anyone want to do this? After all, the high noise levels, the numerous potential distractions, the lack of student engagement, and the sheer volume of students must make this a truly untenable situation. Not so. Teaching the large class can be an extremely rewarding experience for both students and faculty. However, we must remember that the critical factor is not the size of the class, but rather the quality of instruction and design.

WHAT IS LARGE?

It is not easy to give an exact cutoff point for what constitutes a large class. However, there is a noticeable difference in the *feeling* of a class when enrollment exceeds the following:

- 25
- 70
- 150
- 400

The difference is due primarily to the fact that physical room size changes at approximately each of these points. In general, rooms that hold fewer than 25 students will allow for moveable furniture, round table discussion, and such. As you move to the next level, the seating tends to be fixed, with front-facing rows with a shared desk. As you approach 100 students to a room, the number of rows will double. Larger rooms may have several sections and may be tiered. Tablet-arm desks are common. Finally, at the largest room size, there will be multiple tiered sections with a staging area for the instructor at the front. Each of these changes in physical space entails a change in psychological space. If you feel that you can no longer do some of the things you would like to do in class, if you feel that assessment has become difficult, or even that you have trouble getting to know the students, that is when the class will feel large to you.

MYTHS SURROUNDING THE LARGE CLASS

Reece McGee (1991) has discussed some of the difficulties and rewards associated with the large class. Here are some of the most pervasive myths.

Large Classes Are Inherently Inferior to Small Classes

Think back to your own undergraduate education. I'm sure that you will remember some excellent large classes and some mediocre small classes. A large class size does not necessarily equate to poor quality instruction. Obviously, there are many things you will have to do differently, but students can be engaged in any size classroom. The trick is to make sure we take the time to accomplish this.

Large Classes Cannot Be Taught Well

McGee (1991) suggests that this myth stems from the observation that large classes often are not taught well. As mentioned earlier, it is more difficult to teach a larger class. Indeed, Bedard and Kuhn (2008) report a consistently large, negative impact of class size on student ratings of teaching across a wide variety of economics courses over a period of five years. Large class instructors received poorer ratings than their colleagues who taught smaller classes. There are many possible reasons for this observation (including factors unrelated to class size per se), but at the very least it lends support to the belief of poorer quality education with large classes.

Good Large Class Instructors Are Merely Entertainers (And They Are Born with this Ability)

This may be the most damaging myth of all. First of all, there is nothing wrong with teaching in a manner that is entertaining. In fact, I would argue that it is essential to be "entertaining" in an extremely large class in order to maximize attention. A problem arises, however, if entertainment is the only goal—stage presence must go hand-in-hand with pedagogy in order to be effective. Second, this is not an issue of nature versus nurture. Some people are a bit better in front of a large audience, but this does not imply that we should select our large-class instructors according to their acting ability. There are many skills that we can all acquire in order to be more effective in the classroom.

PROS AND CONS

In addition to the myths, McGee (1991) also comments on various advantages and disadvantages with respect to the large class. Let's begin with the disadvantages.

Student Anonymity. In a large class, you will not be able to identify all students by name. In fact, you may have difficulty even seeing some of the students at the back of the classroom. Thus, students may feel that they are anonymous. Apart from the fact that we do not want students to feel that they are only "numbers" in the classroom, anonymity can generate classroom management problems. When individuals feel anonymous, they are more likely to follow the lead of others (Postmes et al. 2001), engage in riskier behavior including cheating (Staub 1996), and not contribute as much to group projects (North, Linley, and Hargreaves 2000). The large-class instructor must attempt to counter anonymity by individualizing students as much as possible.

Low Cognitive Level. There is a tendency to believe that in a large class you must teach to the lowest common denominator—bring down the level of instruction in order to reach everyone. There is some evidence suggesting that this does happen (Cote and Allahar 2007), but it is not inevitable. Instructors must strive to keep the bar at a reasonable level—students want to be challenged in the university setting and we must continue to present that level of challenge.

Low Motivation to Achieve. In every classroom there are a certain number of students who will do well no matter what the instructor does, and a certain number who will do poorly. But there is also a group in the middle who could do better if they had some extra attention. In my large class, this could be as many as 400 students. Clearly, the instructor must provide a way for students to get this extra help, without creating a workload crisis.

On the positive side, there are a few advantages as well.

Exposure to the Best Instructors. Universities can make the decision to put the best instructors in front of the largest classes. In this way, the greatest number of students can be exposed to the best professors. While this is a laudable suggestion, few universities actually have this in place as an explicit policy. In addition, we must consider a host of other issues that follow from this suggestion. For example, how do we define "best"? Do we have to take away resources from senior courses in order to achieve this? How does this impact a faculty member's workload?

Cost Effective. Departments and faculties can save money by offering larger classes. In fact, this is one of the main reasons we have large classes at the first-year level. But make no mistake about this, large classes cannot be cheaply run. If proper funding is not in place to support the large class (teaching assistants, equipment, etc.), engagement will falter and students will be disadvantaged. There is an enormous amount of effort that goes into making a large class work and this must be recognized.

THE AUDIENCE–PERFORMER MODEL

Whether we want to believe it or not, whether we want to accept it or not, it is difficult to avoid the fact that teaching in a large-class setting is a performance. This is driven by the venue in which we teach (a lecture "theater") and the room dynamics. All of the students are aligned in rows fading into the distance (much like an audience in a theater), and the instructor is at the front, either on stage or in a "pit." The appropriate analogy here is not so much instructor–learner as it is audience–performer, and we must learn to embrace this theater metaphor. There are many elements we might consider, but let's examine a few in detail.

Set

A set is a facade, a structure created on stage to make the audience think that they are in a particular location. Sets project a sense of time and space and add realism to the performance. Often, we walk into a classroom and simply accept the set left there by the previous instructor. This may include pieces of equipment left at the front of the room, old handouts, chairs, and perhaps, garbage. This is, most likely, not the set you want to construct. Whenever possible, move equipment and furniture you do not plan to use, tidy up the teaching space, and make it work for you. If not, you will play your part against the unintentional set created for you.

Ambiance

Think about what it feels like to enter a theater (live or film). Are all the room lights on? Is there a flurry of activity at the front of the room? Typically, no. As you enter a theater, the lights are dimmed somewhat, the stage is set, and there is some pleasant music playing. It is a comfortable place to be. By contrast, a lecture hall is brightly lit, the stage is in transition from one instructor to the next, and it is anything but comfortable. We can change this to make the classroom a more user-friendly environment. Dim some of the lights. Set up early if you can and even play music if you like. Lecture halls do not have to be sterile and uninviting.

Equipment

All theaters use equipment to present the performance. The same is true for the large classroom. Much of the equipment is hidden in wall racks and you just need to become familiar with the procedures involved to turn on the stuff you want and switch the sources. While no one will expect you to repair things if they break, you should know how to perform routine tasks, such as rebooting the computer, attaching a laptop, finding spare bulbs or batteries, and so on. In addition, know who to call when something breaks and you do need professional help. Finally, have a backup plan.

Performance

If the students are the audience, then we, the lecturers, are the performers. This notion of teaching as a performance art is certainly not new (see Armstrong 2003; Sarason 1999) and forces us to look at *how* we deliver a lecture in the classroom. To engage the audience, you need to move around the classroom, make eye contact with as many students as possible, modulate your voice, and learn how to use the microphone appropriately. One of the best ways to improve your classroom performance is to have a colleague watch while you teach and critique your behavior. It is also a good idea to record your teaching on tape or disc. It should be noted that variation in these types of nonverbal behaviors is not simply related to instructor evaluations. Murray (1997) has shown that these techniques actually lead to greater student learning.

IS LECTURING ALL I CAN DO?

Although the lecture is the default teaching strategy in the large class, there are other approaches you can adopt. In fact, many would argue that some of these methods must be included in your class in order to actively involve the students. This not meant to be a definitive list, but rather a sampling of a few techniques that I have actually used in classes of over 1,000 students.

Questions

Asking questions is an important part of any university class. One may think that this would be difficult in a large class due to student anonymity, lack of involvement, or even potential embarrassment on behalf of the students. However, it is relatively easy to generate questions in class—all you have to do is encourage the behavior. I tell my students that they should ask questions, both in and out of class. If we cannot get to a question in class (and this does happen), they can email the question to me or one of the teaching assistants. I hold informal office hours before and after class. Finally, students can also write a question on a piece of paper and drop it into a large "Question Box" at the front of the room. I review these questions after every class and discuss the important or frequently asked ones at the beginning of the next lecture.

Demonstrations

Doing a demonstration in a large class takes a bit of planning, but it can have quite a large impact. Whenever possible, I try to involve the entire class. For example, I may do a mini-experiment, where one side of the class gets one set of instructions and the other side gets a different set. We then compare the results from both groups. The entire class may be given a homework assignment (e.g., keep a dream journal) to be discussed at a later point in the course. At other times, I will use "volunteers" from the audience (e.g., for a memory task). Demonstrations such as these not only increase engagement and promote active learning, but also serve to reduce anonymity and promote a sense of class cohesiveness.

Buzz Groups

This is an active learning technique in which small groups (two to four students) are asked to talk to each other about a particular topic for a few minutes. Following the discussion, groups share what they have talked about. A variant of this model is "think–pair–share," where students first think about an issue, then discuss it with one other person, and finally, share the pair's views with another pair. Either can be set up easily in a large class, but there are three important caveats. First, you must choose the topic carefully. People can discuss anything, but you want this to be a topic that produces a variety of opinions. Second, there will be a lot of noise generated in a large class—make sure you have a method for regaining control. Finally, it is important that most students have a way of expressing what they buzzed about. Consider using some form of selection (e.g., "Let's hear from section five today") and possibly allow other sections to post comments to a discussion board.

The One-Minute Paper

This is a great method to get feedback on your teaching and for assessing what your students have learned. At the end of class, simply ask student to take one minute and write down comments on a particular topic. This could be an exam-type question, a survey of opinion, and so forth. Variations on this method include the one-word essay (tell me the most important thing you learned today) or the muddiest point (write down what you had difficulty understanding). As with other active learning techniques, you must discuss these responses with students and perhaps provide a venue for students to share their thoughts.

Quescussion

This is a discussion technique devised by Paul Bidwell at the University of Saskatchewan. It is especially useful when dealing with difficult and emotion-laden topics. There are a few simple rules: questions only (no statements); you must be civil; no fake questions (e.g., "That's a weak point, isn't it?"); at least two other students must speak before you can speak again (the actual number can be changed); and finally, the class monitors and enforces all the rules. Note that the role of the instructor in this method is simply to introduce the topic. After that, she or he does not comment on the process until the end. This method allows students to speak about the topic without having to own a comment. So I could ask a controversial question without having to say that I hold a certain viewpoint. Note that the instructor should keep a record of all questions asked and summarize the points in the next class. Watch for any inaccurate beliefs expressed in the quescussion and be prepared to address these issues.

ENCOURAGING ENGAGEMENT THROUGH TECHNOLOGY

For the most part, the suggestions previously presented can be employed without the use of technology. One can create even more engaging possibilities by using technology that exists in many of our large classrooms.

Facebook

While many of us use a course web site powered by a classroom management tool such as WebCT, it is easy to set up a Facebook site as well. The advance of a social networking site is twofold. First, most students are familiar with Facebook and use it on a regular basis. It is also much more user-friendly than closed course sites. Note that you should never post any confidential material to a Facebook site precisely because it is open. Second, Facebook allows for easy sharing of material among the members of the group. Students can post photos, links to video, and so on quite easily. This does require a bit of monitoring to ensure that only appropriate materials are posted. Nonetheless, it is a good way of informally presenting topics to the whole class.

Chats

Whether you use the course site or another product, chat rooms and discussion boards provide an opportunity for students to continue classroom conversation beyond class. But you might consider running a chat during class. If your classroom is wireless enabled and you have teaching assistant (TA) who can monitor the activity, have students log on to the chat during class. In this manner, students can ask questions to the TA in real time, discuss topics when assigned, or simply ask for clarification of an issue. I have used this in my class of 800 and we run a real time chat for exam review the entire day before an exam. Students report that both types of chats are helpful. This also builds a classroom community and allows the instructor to make use of the wireless capability existing in the room.

TIPS

There are numerous suggestions we could close with. Here are my top ten for large class instruction.

1. **Pedagogy First.** Whatever you do in class, always have student learning in mind. If you use discussion, what is the goal? If you show a video, how does this help to understand the concept? Structure your presentation around clear learning outcomes and add the methods as appropriate.

2. **Do Not Talk about Topics You Know "Nothing" About.** This seems like an obvious suggestion—one would not discuss the fine points of nuclear physics in a poetry class (unless you were

a physicist discussing poetry on the topic). However, we are often lead down this path when students ask questions. In an effort to save face, we might attempt to answer a question without all the relevant information. Ultimately, you will stumble with this approach. The better technique is to admit you do not know the answer, but you will find out. Not only is this intellectually honest, but it also provides an academic model for the students.

3. **Things Will Fail; Try To Be Ready.** No matter how well you prepare for class and how much you check all the equipment, something will go wrong. Batteries run out. Audio systems fail. Computers get viruses. Trying to solve an equipment problem in front of several hundred students can be disconcerting and if it goes on too long, you will lose the class. Have a back-up plan in place from the beginning. Also be sure to check your classroom at the beginning of the year and after any long break—these are times when the equipment tends to be serviced and may be unplugged when you return.

4. **Redundancy Is a Virtue.** We often think it is a bad idea to repeat ourselves, but in class this is a worthwhile strategy. Repetition of concepts and examples stresses their importance and gives students a chance to catch up with you. Note: Do not simply repeat the same thing over and over, give several different examples and rephrase the central concept.

5. **Use All the Technology You Can.** As mentioned earlier, you can encourage engagement by facilitating the submission of questions, using a course web site, and using other Web tools (such as chatting) to build a class community. Students are tuned in to technology and the Web (Atkinson 2006)—this is the best way to reach them.

6. **Over-prepare.** People often ask how much time one should spend in preparation for a class. The rule for people who do professional presentations is twenty to one—twenty hours prep time for every hour of talk. I realize that this seems extreme in an academic environment, but the point remains that a polished talk requires this degree of preparation. You may not spend twenty hours on every lecture, and you may spend more

time on some. The bottom line is: time on task is as important here as anywhere else.

7. **Attend to Your Nonverbal Behavior.** Remember that lectures are performances and we can improve our abilities through observation and practice.

8. **Whatever Works for 20 Students May Not Work for 100 or 500.** Again, this seems obvious. Discussion is harder to do (but not impossible) in a large class than in a small one. However, this rule also applies to other elements of class. Overheads work in a small classroom, but not as well in a lecture theater. You do not need a microphone for a class of 30, but it is essential in a class of 200. If you have any doubts about what will work, have a colleague listen to you teach and give you an opinion.

9. **Structure Everything. Success in the Large Class Hinges on Organization and Structure.** Well-organized classes flow smoothly, and highly structured courses do not generate ambiguity. Have clear expectations about everything from due dates to classroom behavior. Put these expectations in your course outline.

10. **Enjoy What You Do.** Teaching the large class can be one of the most rewarding activities of your university career, but not if you find that it is a constant burden. Try to identify what the problem areas are and seek help if you need it.

REFERENCES

Armstrong, Paul. 2003. *Teaching as stand-up comedy: The metaphor of scripted and improvised performance of teaching.* Paper presented at SCUTREA, 33rd annual conference, University of Wales, Bangor, July.

Atkinson, Michael L. 2006. Advice for (and from) the young at heart: Understanding the millennial generation. *Guidance & Counselling,* 19(4): 153–157.

Bedard, Kelly, and Peter Kuhn. 2008. Where class size really matters: Class size and student ratings of instructor effectiveness. *Economics of Education Review,* 27(3): 253–265.

Cote, James E., and Anton L. Allahar. 2007. *Ivory tower blues: A university system in crisis.* Toronto, Canada: University of Toronto Press.

McGee, Reece. 1991. *Handling hordes: Teaching large classes.* West Lafayette, IN: Continuing Education Office, Purdue University.

Murray, Harry G. 1997. Effective teaching behaviors in the college classroom. In Raymond P. Perry and John C. Smart, *Effective teaching in higher education: Research and practice* (pp. 171–204). New York: Agathon Press.

North, Adrian C., P. Alex Linley, and David J. Hargreaves. 2000. Social loafing in a co-operative classroom task. *Educational Psychology, 20*(4): 389–392.

Postmes, Tom, Russell Spears, Khaled Sakhel, and Daphne de Groot. 2001. Social influence in computer-mediated communication: The effects of anonymity on group behavior. *Personality and Social Psychology Bulletin, 27*(10): 1243–1253.

Sarason, Seymour B. 1999. *Teaching as a performing art.* New York: Teachers College Press.

Staub, Ervin. 1996. Cultural-society roots of violence: The examples of genocidal violence and of contemporary youth violence in the United States. *American Psychologist, 51*(2): 117–132.

The Inquiry Circle

Jeanette McDonald
Wilfrid Laurier University, Ontario

It must be remembered that the purpose of education is not to fill
the minds of students with facts ... it is to teach them to think, if
that is possible, and always to think for themselves.
Robert Hutchins (1936, 8)

WHAT IS AN INQUIRY CIRCLE?

An inquiry circle (IC) provides a flexible forum to actively engage students with the subject matter and support student learning in a meaningful, intentional way that is discussion based. In practice it can take several forms, serve various academic goals, and be adapted to multiple disciplines and physical contexts. More than just a classroom structure, IC is also a teaching and learning approach that is premised on a set of design principles. They are listed next.

1. **Makes Learning Transparent.** So often the "how" of learning can be a mystery to students. In many cases, students may think they're on the right track in their learning and studying approach (i.e., they know the material) only to discover on a test or an assignment that they are drawing a blank or having difficulty applying the so-called "learned" material to new situations. Demystifying the "how" of learning by modeling the inquiry process (i.e., by word and deed) in class and providing opportunities to practice and receive feedback is essential to the IC process. Metacognitively, it also helps students gain awareness of how they learn and what they need to do to learn in a given discipline or context.

2. **Reflects the Inquiry Process of the Discipline.** Each discipline has its own values, its own language to communicate ideas and

69

practices, and, most importantly, its own set of approaches to solving problems and critically studying or examining issues and dilemmas. Yet how often do we consciously and clearly communicate to students how someone in our discipline (e.g., a geographer) thinks, writes, or solves problems? The IC approach provides a means to do just this (i.e., model and practice how someone in their discipline thinks, writes, solves problems, and makes meaning).

3. **Constructs Knowledge Collaboratively.** A constructivist approach to learning accepts that knowledge is socially constructed, that is, people make meaning together (Bruffee 1993; Matthews 1996). Therefore, learning not only involves individual effort (e.g., critical reflection, individual preparation), but collective effort as well. In this view, the professor is no longer "informing" students about the content alone (though there will be times when this is warranted), but "facilitating" and "participating" in the learning process, not to mention "constructing" the learning environment (i.e., designing and structuring the IC).

4. **Develops Knowledge and Skills.** The goal of the process and product of IC should be the development of specific knowledge and skills at the appropriate taxonomic level (e.g., cognitive, affective, psychomotor; see http://www.nwlink.com/~donclark/hrd/bloom.html). Ideally, this should be done not only for the subject matter at hand, but also the course, discipline, and academic program as a whole.

5. **Physical Arrangement Supports the Process.** Whatever form IC takes, its physical arrangement (e.g., discussion circle) and membership (e.g., pairs, small/large groups) should facilitate and justify student learning and discussion and minimize distracters (e.g., power struggles or student conflicts).

These five principles provide the basis for designing a meaningful IC experience that supports specific academic goals and structures.

IC AND THE PROFESSOR

Designing an IC experience requires you to think differently about how you approach teaching and learning and how you structure contact time with your students. There is less focus on content delivery alone (i.e., what you do), and more focus on designing and providing meaningful learning experiences for your students that actively engages them with the subject matter. Therefore, your role changes from one of strictly "sage on the stage" to "guide on the side." Here are some examples of what this means for you.

- Modeling the desired learning process (e.g., articulate the steps associated with solving a mathematical problem or reading critically)
- Scaffolding student learning (e.g., provide learning hooks or frameworks on which to structure and build student knowledge and understanding of course material)
- Providing opportunities for students to practice and receive feedback on their knowledge and skill development
- Designing pre- and post-exercises (e.g., before/during/after class) to prepare students for IC exercises/experiences (e.g., read a text and submit discussion questions)
- Developing worksheets or forms to guide (e.g., probing, open-ended questions) and document (e.g., tables or matrices) student learning
- Accounting for the maturity and skill level of students when staging and setting the complexity of an IC experience
- Allowing for multiple experiences and perspectives in the design of IC experiences

THE IC AND THE STUDENT

Likewise, an IC approach requires students to work differently than expected in a traditional lecture-based course. To maximize their experience, students need to do the following:

- Actively engage with the course material and their fellow peers to develop knowledge, skill, and understanding
- Move from receiver to cocreator of their own knowledge and understanding
- Take responsibility for and manage their own learning (e.g., time on task)
- View their professor both as an expert and colearner

- Prepare in advance for the IC activity as determined by the professor

IC PHYSICAL ARRANGEMENTS

The physical arrangement of the learning environment should likewise support the IC learning experience. As IC activities are discussion based, students should ideally be arranged so they can see and hear one another (Cameron 1999). Even in a lecture hall where furniture is bolted to the floor and seating is arranged in rows, students can physically move themselves to engage one another. The following figures provide examples of different physical arrangements that can be used to support an IC experience, whether it's a one-time learning task or an ongoing, multisession learning activity.

The simplest of arrangements is a grouping of chairs or desks in a single circle (or several circles, depending on room size and capacity). This formation can easily be used for a discussion circle or team assignment (see Figure 1).

A more complex arrangement may consist of concentric circles where chairs, desks, or workstations are positioned in an inner and outer circle (Figures 2a and 2b). Barkley, Cross, and Major's (2005) example of *think-aloud pair problem solving*, discussed in the following list, lends well to this setup.

In a large classroom setting where the furniture is arranged in rows, students can be divided into pairs, triads, or groups of four with relative ease simply by turning to a peer seated to either side, in front, or behind them, again in a circular pattern, to achieve the learning task (Figure 3).

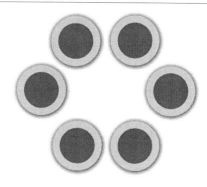

Figure 1. Single circle.

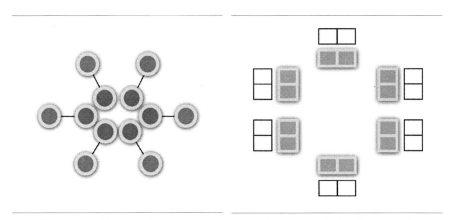

Figure 2a. Concentric circle.   Figure 2b. Paired/grouped
                                     concentric circles.

Again, Barkley, Cross, and Major's (2005) example of a *send-a-problem* activity may work well in this type of physical arrangement.

DESIGNING IC ACTIVITIES: GETTING STARTED

An IC experience can be designed to be a discreet one-time activity (e.g., send-a-problem), or it can be part of a larger classroom structure that is ongoing (e.g., case study analysis), where each successive activity or exercise builds upon the next in an ever-more-complex set of related activities. For first time users, the former is less risky and the easier of the two to begin experimentation.

Barkley, Cross, and Major (2005) describe a number of collaborative learning techniques in their book that lend themselves to the IC approach and its associated design principles. Two examples from their book are briefly described next, along with a few design notes. Both can be adapted to a variety of disciplines.

Think-Aloud Pair Problem Solving (TAPPS)

For this activity, one student (Student A) reads aloud and works through a problem, recording their solution step-by-step on a piece of paper. While working through the solution, Student A voices aloud their thinking process (i.e., their reasoning for each step), while a second student (Student B) listens in an attempt to understand the reasoning of Student A. When Student A needs help, Student B may additionally serve to remind Stu-

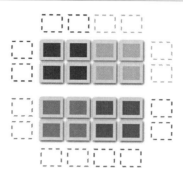

Figure 3. Grouped circles in rows.

dent A of the discipline-specific problem-solving steps, ask for clarification, or make a suggestion (but not solve the problem). Following completion of the problem, Students A and B may further discuss the answer and the problem-solving process (including any missteps) until consensus is achieved and both students are satisfied that they understand the how and why of the problem and its solution (e.g., Why did Student A use this rule or equation versus another? Could the problem have been solved another way?).

Both open-ended and single-answer questions are appropriate for this kind of activity, though the latter is more common. Each student should take a turn solving a different problem. To help document the learning process, devise a worksheet such as the one found in Appendix A. Note that this activity is intended to emphasize the process versus the product of problem solving.

Send-a-Problem

For this activity, students work in teams (e.g., two to six students) to solve a problem or dilemma (e.g., mathematical, scenario-based). Each team (Group A) has a set amount of time to work through the problem and record their answer and reasoning process (whether completed or not) on a worksheet (much like the one found in Appendix A), before passing it on to another team (Group B). Group B starts fresh (no peaking at the worksheet of Group A) with the same problem as Group A, following the same completion process. Once the time period is up, Group B passes their worksheet (along with Group A's) to a third team (Group C) who evaluates the worksheets, synthesizes the information, and adds any additional data that may be needed. The process ends with an oral report from each evaluating team, during which the best solution is presented, any misinformation or problem-solving errors are addressed, and correct processes and solutions are shared.

Open-ended questions and problems work best with this activity. Make sure to design enough problem sets (questions/scenarios/cases) and work packages appropriate for the class size and the number of rounds a problem is to be reviewed (minimum two work rounds and one evaluation round for a total of three teams per problem). See Appendix B for a sample setup and schedule. Ideally, each work package should contain a copy of the problem/dilemma/scenario, enough worksheets for each team to document their problem-solving process and solution, and a master worksheet to guide the final team in the evaluation and presentation process. For larger classes, devise a strategy to identify teams and distribute packages between streamed work groups (I've used playing cards in classes as large as 200 for just such an activity). Consider using this activity in preparation for an exam using past test questions. Note that this activity is intended to aid in the development of effective problem-solving skills as well as the ability to compare and discriminate among multiple solutions.

IC IN ACTION

An alternate approach to the two examples previously listed is to build an IC experience around a set of questions that actively engage students while developing their knowledge and understanding of course content. McKeachie (1994), for example, describes three types of questions to do just this: comparative, connective, and critical. The first requires students to compare and contrast different perspectives, theories, and approaches. The second asks students to dig beyond the surface and make connections between or within the subject matter. The third directs students to question and probe the validity of a specific assertion or interpretation.

Anne Charles, a professor at Conestoga College in Kitchener, Ontario, uses an IC-type approach in her teaching. For example, in her Contemporary Social Problems and Introduction to Social Sciences courses, students work together in teams to complete a series of questions associated with lecture, text, and media materials currently under study. The complexity (i.e., level of higher-order thinking) of questions asked increases with each unit of study and are directly aligned with the unit outcomes outlined in the course syllabus. The unit assignments, while only worth two percent each, over the course of the semester, comprise twenty percent of the students' total grade. More important, the assignments actively engage her students with the material at hand in a meaningful way; provide a mechanism to document and assess their learning; prepare them for the kinds of questions they may encounter on their exams; and present a springboard for larger class discussion. Class time is provided for students to discuss, debate, reflect, and record their responses. Students work in the same teams throughout the term (see figures one and three for their physical arrangements) and submit their team worksheets in a group folder. These worksheets offer valuable insight into the students' learning (which can be used to modify unit lessons/lectures) and provide a basis to supply weekly feedback to each team on their progress to date. Sample questions from different unit assignments are listed next. As the questions become more complex, the number of questions asked per assignment decreases.

- **Unit 2 (Introduction to Social Sciences).** What are the strengths and weaknesses of the ideas of Smith, Marx, and Keynes on economics? Do their arguments still have relevance today?

- **Unit 3 (Contemporary Social Problems).** Using the conflict perspective, explain why tobacco is legal and heroin is not? (Students are asked similar questions in the same assignment using different theoretical perspectives.)

- **Unit 9 (Contemporary Social Problems).** Oscar Lewis (1998, 9) noted that "some see the poor as virtuous, upright, serene, independent, honest, secure, kind, simple, and happy, while others see them as evil, mean, violent, sordid, and criminal." Which view of the poor do you tend to hold? How have various social influences, such as parents, peers, media, social class, and education, shaped your views toward the poor?

Option: Professor Charles's IC assignment could be adapted to the send-a-problem exercise outlined by Barkley, Cross, and Major (2005), as described earlier.

CLOSING REMINDERS

Keep in mind that the learning process, like the physical arrangement, is circular. See for example, Kolb's experiential learning model and others at: http://reviewing.co.uk/research/learning.cycles.htm.

Inquiry-based approaches embrace many tasks, including asking questions, researching information and generating ideas/solutions, discussing, interpreting, reflecting, and deliberating findings toward a shared understanding of the issue or topic at hand (Jarrett 1997). Refer to McMaster University's inquiry-based approach to learning for more information: http://www.mcmaster.ca/cll/inquiry/whats.unique.about.inquiry.htm. See also the "For Further Reflection and Action" section at the end of the book for more advice on using IC in your class.

ACKNOWLEDGMENTS

Many thanks to Professor Anne Charles for agreeing to share her teaching materials and ideas for inclusion in this article.

APPENDIX A: PROBLEM-SOLVING WORKSHEET

Instructions: Use column A to record your step-by-step process (solution set) for solving the provided problem (e.g., numerical steps). Use column B to record your reasoning/logic (including questions and resources consulted) used to derive your answer for each step in column A. (e.g., I chose the following theory/equation to answer this problem set because …).

COLUMN A: SOLUTION SET	COLUMN B: REASONING/LOGIC

APPENDIX B: SAMPLE PROBLEM-SOLVING AND EVALUATION SCHEDULE

	Stage 1: Problem solving		Stage 2: Solution evaluation
	Time frame 1	Time frame 2	Time frame 3
Group A	Solve problem 1	Solve problem 2	Evaluate solutions for problem 3
Group B	Solve problem 2	Solve problem 3	Evaluate solutions for problem 1
Group C	Solve problem 3	Solve problem 1	Evaluate solutions for problem 2

Note: This table assumes there are three problems/scenarios being reviewed by teams of students at the same time. Time permitting and as appropriate, you may have more than two rounds of problem solving (Barkley et al. 2005, 180).

REFERENCES

Barkley, Elizabeth F., Patricia K. Cross, and Claire H. Major. 2005. *Collaborative learning techniques: A handbook for college faculty.* San Francisco: Jossey-Bass.

Bruffee, Kenneth. 1993. *Collaborative learning: Higher education, interdependence, and the authority of knowledge.* Baltimore, MD: Johns Hopkins University Press.

Cameron, Beverly. 1999. *Active learning.* Green Guide No. 2. Halifax, Nova Scotia, Canada: Society for Teaching and Learning in Higher Education.

Hutchins, Robert. 1936. What is a university? (Radio address, April 18, 1935, Parent–Teachers Association). In *No friendly voice* (pp. 5–11). Chicago: University of Chicago Press.

Jarrett, Denise. 1997. *Inquiry strategies for science and mathematics learning. It's just good teaching.* Portland, OR: Northwest Regional Education Laboratory, http:// www.nwrel.org/msec/images/resources/justgood/05.97.pdf.

Lewis, Oscar. 1998. The culture of poverty. *Society*, 35(2), 7–9.

Matthews, Roberta. 1996. Collaborative learning: Creating knowledge with students. In Robert J. Menges, Maryellen Weimer, and Associates (Eds.), *Teaching on solid ground: Using scholarship to improve practice* (pp. 101–124). San Francisco: Jossey-Bass.

McKeachie, Wilbert. 1994. *Teaching tips: Strategies, research and theory for college and university teachers.* Lexington, MA: D.C. Heath.

OTHER RECOMMENDED RESOURCES

Brookfield, Stephen, and Stephen Preskill. 1999. *Discussion as a way of teaching: Tools and techniques for democratic collaborative learning classrooms.* San Francisco: Jossey-Bass.

Davis, Barbara. 1993. *Tools for teaching.* San Francisco: Jossey-Bass.

Kustra, Erika, and Michael Potter. 2007. *Leading effective discussions.* Green Guide No. 9. Hamilton, Ontario, Canada: Society for Teaching and Learning in Higher Education.

Millis, Barbara, and Phillip Cottell. 1998. *Cooperative learning for higher education faculty.* (American Council on Education Oryx Press Series on Higher Education). Phoenix, AZ: Oryx Press.

Nilson, Linda. 1998. *Teaching at its best: A research-based resource for college instructors.* Bolton, MA: Anker.

Silberman, Melvin. 1996. *Active learning: 101 strategies to teach any subject.* Needham Heights, MA: Allyn and Bacon.

Part Three

Engaging Students with New Technologies

Blog or Discussion Board
Which Is the Right Tool to Choose?

Matt Crosslin

University of Texas at Arlington

Blogs and discussion boards have become important educational tools, both in hybrid courses that mix technology with face-to-face learning as well as in completely online courses. Blogs, a relatively new tool, are sometimes heralded as the savior of education—a way to look "cool" to your students at the same time you are getting them to think critically. Some instructors have even begun using blogs in place of a course management system (CMS). Discussion boards have been around slightly longer and have become fairly standard in online learning for promoting active discussion. Considering that some feel there is really no basic difference between a blog and a discussion board, instructors many wonder if blogs and discussion boards can be used interchangeably or if there is a time and place for each of them.

BLOGS AND DISCUSSION BOARDS: THE SAME BUT STILL DIFFERENT

The truth of the matter is that there are probably as many similarities between both tools as there are differences. To some, the similarities and differences are just a matter of personal opinion. To others, the differences are major points of contention. The best way to approach these two educational tools is to be aware of how they are similar and then examine the differences to help determine which one is the best tool for a specific activity.

On a basic level, blogs and discussion boards are both similar in that they are forms of communicating with a group of people through self-publication. Some type of event encourages the genesis of new material. This event may be a current news story, a classroom assignment, or anything else the author considers educationally valid. The author inputs content in to an online program designed to publish their ideas or questions and then submits the content for feedback from their readers. Depending on which software tool is used as an interface, readers can review new content by subscribing to RSS (RDF Site Summary) feeds, choosing to receive email updates, or visiting the web site directly at any time they choose. These web sites may be password protected or open to all visitors.

The actual factor that makes blogs and discussion boards different is the focus. The focus of a blog is different than the focus of a discussion board. For blogs, the focus is on the most recent blog entry in a series of entries. For discussion boards, the focus is on the response to an initial discussion question. These differing foci will also cause differences in the way that the interface and feedback of each tool are practically used. Because of these differences, educators need to carefully consider which tool to use when considering either one for a course activity.

Since the focus of blogging is on the most recent entry, the interface of the blog will display the entries in reverse chronological order, with the most recent entry on top. Feedback is in the form of comments, hidden behind a link at the top or bottom of the post. Commenting systems usually only allow for feedback on the blog post (and not on other comments), so discussions that occur in blog comment sections are typically more difficult to follow.

Discussion boards usually focalize on replies to an initial question. Therefore, discussion boards will have an interface that brings attention to the newest replies. Sometimes the new posts (usually called threads) are highlighted, sometimes threads with newer replies are put at the top of a list of all threads, and sometimes a symbol is placed next to the thread with new content. Discussion boards also typically have a "quote" feature that encourages readers to comment on each others comments. Some discussion programs, such as phpBB (http://www. phpbb.com), even allow for threaded comments, where replies are grouped with the content being referenced (see Figure 1).

All of these tactics are designed to encourage discussion. According to Kassop (2003, 1), discussion boards generate higher quality responses because "students have the opportunity to post well-considered comments without the demands of the immediate, anxiety-producing F2F discus-

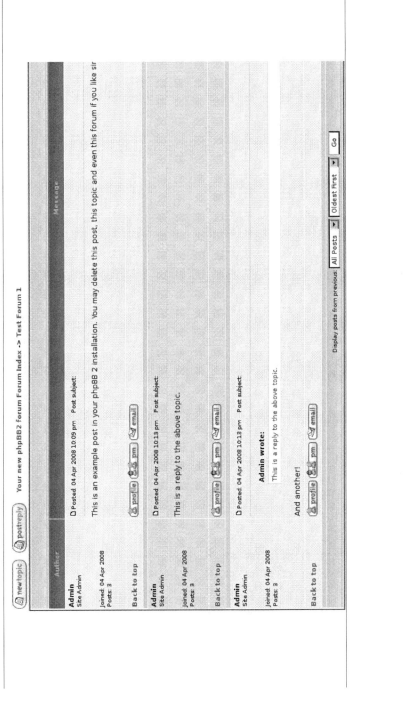

newtopic **postreply** Your new phpBB2 forum Forum Index -> Test Forum 1

Author	Message
Admin Site Admin Joined: 04 Apr 2008 Posts: 3	Posted 04 Apr 2008 10:09 pm Post subject: This is an example post in your phpBB 2 installation. You may delete this post, this topic and even this forum if you like sir
Back to top	**profile** **pm** **email**
Admin Site Admin Joined: 04 Apr 2008 Posts: 3	Posted 04 Apr 2008 10:13 pm Post subject: This is a reply to the above topic.
Back to top	**profile** **pm** **email**
Admin Site Admin Joined: 04 Apr 2008 Posts: 3	Posted 04 Apr 2008 10:13 pm Post subject: **Admin wrote:** This is a reply to the above topic. And another!
Back to top	**profile** **pm** **email**

Display posts from previous: All Posts ▼ Oldest First ▼ Go

sion, which often elicits the first response that comes to mind rather than the best possible response."

CHOOSING THE RIGHT TOOL FOR AN EDUCATIONAL ACTIVITY

Knowing the differences between blogs and discussion boards can be helpful to educators who want to decide which tool to use in an educational activity. Blogs focus on the most recent input entry itself. If your activity needs to focus on a larger amount of information being presented by one person or a group, then a blog is the way to go. Presenting information can be accomplished by many other means, so you want to make sure that the information being presented will also need updating on a regular basis. If you want some feedback on this information, blogs can still be used for your activity as long as the feedback is in the form of comments that relate back to the original information.

If you want to focus on a discussion about a specific question or set of questions, then a discussion board is the way to go. Typically with discussion boards, the initial input is a question that starts a discussion. This discussion may or may not lead to topics that are totally unrelated to the original question. If you want your students to collaborate to create an answer or come to their own conclusions about a topic, then a discussion board is the tool to choose.

Krause (2004) published an online essay that looks at some of the mistakes he made when first using blogs in education. His course used an email list for discussion instead of an actual discussion program, but his insights in to the differences between blogs and discussion groups give addition information about these two tools, as well as tips for how to use both effectively.

Practically speaking, students are usually interested in where they can find the "answer." As an instructor, think of it this way: In a blog, the answer is found in the initial post. For discussion boards, the answer is found in the feedback or replies to the original question.

WHEN A BLOG IS NOT A BLOG

Discussion boards are generally used for discussion in most courses. Occasionally, someone will use a discussion board as a blog—focusing on a long initial input of information and then squelching or totally shutting down any discussion. These cases are rare. More often, if a tool is being misused, one will find a blog being used for something other than what it is intended for. A few of these misuses include:

1. **The Blog as Discussion Board.** Some instructors will require that students comment on their blog and then "respond to three other student comments" for full credit on an assignment. To accomplish this, they will use a blog program that probably puts all comments in order, one after another, at the end of the blog post. This makes following comments on other comments very difficult. Not to mention that ongoing "discussions" get buried in the blog as new posts are added. A discussion board still makes the best tool for discussing.

2. **The Blog as CMS or Virtual Learning Environment (Vle).** This use for blogs seems to have gained popularity among do-it-yourself types that dislike some of the more popular existing CMS software (Blackboard, Desire2Learn, etc.). Free online blog web sites seem like an attractive solution, but the blog becomes more of a web page than an activity. Blogs can be used to effectively distribute course content (see the lists of ideas in the Blogging and Learning section below), but they also lack important tools like grade books and automatic enrollment that real CMS/VLE software can offer. As hard as it is to give up control or to use a product that may not totally fit your specific needs, the CMS/VLE application is still the best place for your online educational base. You can also insert links in your CMS/VLE to an outside tool.

3. **The Blog as Project Home Page.** This misuse probably arose in the pre-Web2.0 Internet age, when creating a web page was more of the domain of IT specialists than the everyday student. A "project home page" (Figure 2) is where students place content that they have created as part of a class project (group or solo). The content is not in chronological order or even open for comments. In these cases, the blog is just an easy tool to upload and format content for free.

Many free tools to create web pages have taken over the realm of web content generation, but the use of a blog as a project home page still persists in some corners. Wikis are a much better tool for this type of project. Wikipedia, one of the more popular wikis, defines a wiki as "a collection of

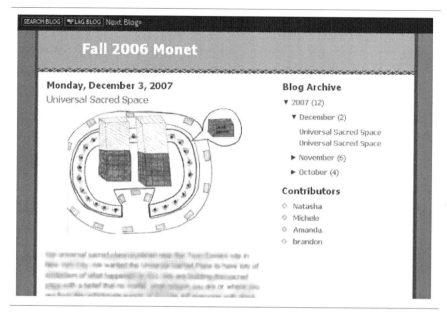

Figure 2. Example of a blog used as a project home page.

web pages designed to enable anyone who accesses it to contribute or modify content, using a simplified markup language . . . often used to create collaborative web sites" (http://en.wikipedia.org/ wiki/Wiki). Wikis are designed to accept collaborative contributions and editing because they make a better tool for project pages than a blog, where content is more often "owned" by the author.

BLOGGING AND LEARNING

Blogs are especially useful in online learning but can also be used to extend learning outside of class time in a face-to-face course. Here are a few ideas for how an instructor could use a blog to model critical thinking:

1. **Current Events Analysis.** Sometimes students need to know how current events relate to the material they are studying. This approach will also help students cut through all of the online clutter that accumulates around a news item and see which ones the instructor deems as appropriate.

2. **Course Reflection.** Students can benefit from the instructor's overall reflections on the progress of the class. This type of blog

could also be a way to look forward to upcoming projects and a way to connect your course with other disciplines.

3. **Theoretical Examples.** Some courses require students to employ higher-order thinking skills in multiple assignments. If this is new to students, they might benefit from seeing how the instructor uses those skills. Keep a running journal of how you critically analyze situations and texts as examples for students.

4. **Cross-discipline Connections.** If several teachers work together on a blog, they could design it in such a way to help students see the bridge between disciplines. For example, the math instructor and the history instructor can blog about how history has been impacted by mathematical discoveries.

These are just a few ideas for an instructor-centric blog. Instructors that are interested in constructivist learning will also probably be interested in having their students keep their own blog. Here are a few ideas for how to use student blogs to foster critical thinking:

1. **Project Reflection.** As students work through a class or a specific project, they can also post a weekly reflective blog entry. These blogs could also be open to the entire class, or students could be put into groups that read and critique each other's posts.

2. **Group Current Event Analysis.** Instead of having the instructor analyze current events, why not have the students perform this task? Students can even be put into groups to help decide what should and should not be posted on the blog.

3. **Promote a Cause.** Students could create a blog that promotes a certain cause or charity (Figure 3). Each week they can blog about something that relates to that cause.

4. **Write a Story.** Each blog entry could be another chapter in an ongoing story. Have students react to a different prompt that you provide each week or have students team together to write an evolving story. One student would write a post and then the other student would take over and write the next chapter. Each blog post has their characters reacting to where the other writer has taken the story.

DISCUSSION AND LEARNING

Using a discussion board in education can be fairly basic—students can always use the board to discuss a topic. Familiarity with discussion boards could lead some activities to become more passive than active. To make discussions more active and critical, restructure discussion board activities to take the discussion in a different direction:

1. **Proctored Debate.** Discussion boards can sometimes descend into a freefall argument, so setting up a discussion board like a proctored debate can help facilitate civil discussion (Figure 4). Even a courtroom-like setup is possible—to try an asynchronous case, for example. Arguments that are presented need to be researched and analyzed, leading to deeper critical thinking.

2. **Brainstorm Session.** Structured brainstorming can work great on a discussion board. The process might take a little longer, but more ideas can be explored in that time.

3. **Feedback Forum.** Students can post work and get feedback from others. Feedback can also be structured to encourage critical thinking. For large classes, this works more efficiently if students are put in to groups.

4. **Classes' Frequently Asked Questions.** Instead of using email for asking questions, why not have students post questions in a discussion forum? Students can answer each other's questions, or ask for further clarification, and then benefit from your response or the responses of other students.

COMBINING BLOGS AND DISCUSSION BOARDS

Some activities will still not fit neatly in to either category. Sometimes blogs and discussion boards need to be combined. Ongoing assignments may entail a large content entry that needs to be the initial focus, but after that the focus might need to shift to a true discussion. Some blog tools allow threaded comment sections that can make this hybrid approach possible. If this is not an option, blog comments can usually be turned off, and a link to a specific discussion board can be embedded at the end of the blog post.

Figure 3. Student blog promoting a cause.

USING OTHER TOOLS

Occasionally, other tools are used in place of a blog, such as wikis, listservs, and CMS programs. Each of these tools has educational benefits—when used in the proper context. Listservs tend to break conversational flow and are therefore hard to follow. So they are usually best used for course announcements and news. Wikis are also excellent tools, but they are better used for group projects where students are constructing a body of information rather than to be used as a blog or discussion board. CMS programs are robust systems that should be used for "big picture" projects and not just blogging.

PRACTICAL ISSUES

Regardless of which tool you choose, you will probably need to set down some guidelines for your students from the beginning. Without some parameters, comments and replies could spiral out of control in no time.

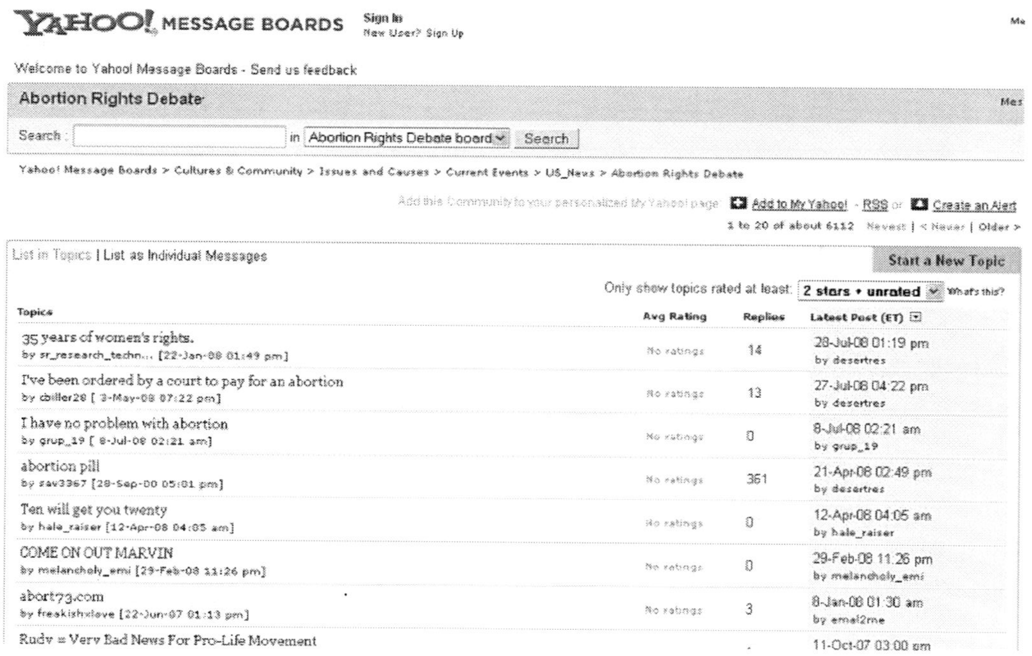

Figure 4. Yahoo discussion board used for a debate

First, remember to set up guidelines for what you consider to be a "minimum acceptable posting" or MAP for each assignment. Rubrics can work great for this. Students need to know that one line responses that basically just say "I agree" will not make the grade on a discussion board. Blog posts will also need a MAP so that students will understand what is expected of them for the project. Maximum limits are also helpful in larger classes or on topics that can go down side tangents. Maximum limits can also help students increase critical thinking by producing more focused postings and responses.

Despite what some may think, netiquette does not come naturally for all students. Because of this, consider setting up some good netiquette guidelines for your students. Emotions and passion are okay, but respect needs to be the foundation of all interactions. Give students some space to learn good manners online, but make sure to have a firm line that has definite consequences once it is crossed.

Another issue you might want to consider when setting up a blog or discussion board is whether or not your assignment should be a public or private venture. Some course subjects are too sensitive to share on the Internet. However, other subjects are ideal for being out in the public arena, where interested parties or even experts in the field can stop by to participate in the conversation or discussion. Students can greatly benefit from public discourse, as long as privacy concerns are properly addressed. Stephen Downes (2004, 1) quotes one school principal describing blogs as a support tool that could be used "to promote reflective analysis and the emergence of a learning community that goes beyond the school walls."

CONCLUSION

Blogs and discussion boards both make excellent tools in learning—when used properly. Neither one is the perfect solution for every situation, so context and pedagogy need to be considered before setting up either one. A properly designed activity containing either tool can work in face-to-face or online classrooms to extend active discussion and critical thinking. See the "For Further Reflection and Action" section at the end of the book for more information on using blogs and discussion boards in your class. The possibilities are endless, so the only way to really go wrong with either tool is not to use them at all.

REFERENCES

Downes, Stephen. 2004. Educational blogging. *EDUCAUSE Review*, 39(5): 14–26. Access at http://connect.educause.edu/Library/EDUCAUSE+Review/Educational Blogging/40493.

Kassop, Mark. 2003. Ten ways online education matches, or surpasses, face-to-face learning. *The Technology Source* (May/June). Access at http://technologysource.org/article/ten_ways_online_education_matches_or_surpasses_facetoface_learning/. See especially reason No. 3: Highly interactive discussions.

Krause, Steven D. 2004. *When blogging goes bad: A cautionary tale about blogs, email lists, discussion, and interaction.* Access at http://english.ttu.edu/kairos/9.1/praxis/krause/.

LiveJournal

Technological Solutions to Traditional Journaling Problems

Margaret D. Anderson

State University of New York at Cortland

Journaling assignments have traditionally been used to encourage students to reflect upon class activities, to express ideas and emotions, or to engage in collaborative construction of new knowledge. Perhaps the most common use of journals is as a way for students to reflect on their own experiences and integrate academic content into their own frame of reference. Phipps (2005, 62) describes various types of journaling, most of which center around self-reflection goals; these include spiritual journals, dream logs, diaries, autobiographies, and memoirs. Other forms of journal writing might include professional journals, interactive reading logs, or theory logs. Whatever the goal of the journaling activity, it has typically been achieved using a notebook format, which brings with it a variety of problems for the student and the instructor. This article describes the use of electronic journaling in a number of different course models and outlines how the use of the LiveJournal Internet program can help to alleviate the problems associated with hard copy journals while maintaining the integrity of the journaling assignments.

TRADITIONAL JOURNALING

Instructors have historically assigned journal writing activities to accomplish a variety of pedagogical goals. Until very recently, all journaling would have used a paper-based medium such as bound notebooks. While writing journal entries in a notebook using a pen or pencil does have the advantages of familiar, low-cost materials and portability, there are also a number of significant problems associated with this format:

- Students need to physically keep track of their journals and they need to be conscious of their handwriting, grammar, and spelling.
- They are limited to creating entries in a sequential manner.
- They cannot revisit a previous entry if they wish to elaborate on it.
- Recording all journal entries in one notebook generally precludes the inclusion of material in other media (video or audio).
- If all entries are contained in the one central repository, it is difficult for students to include private comments not to be shared.

Some faculty have recognized that these private comments are useful for students and have encouraged them to make the entries, then staple over the page when the journal is submitted for review.

Some disadvantages of the notebook journals for faculty are:

- The collection of journals at specified points in the semester (depending on class size) could be physically overwhelming, particularly when faced with reviewing a daunting volume of sometimes obscurely handwritten material at certain times in the semester.
- Physical journals frequently leave limited space for instructors to provide students with crucial feedback, which is also handwritten and often just as difficult to decipher as the original entries.
- Providing feedback at set review points reduces its timeliness and therefore students' ability to incorporate the feedback into subsequent journal entries.
- The periodic collection of hardcopy journals allows students to procrastinate in their journal assignments, often completing the entire series just prior to collection points, thus defeating the purpose of timely reflective writing.
- Entries may also be distorted by the passage of time to the point where they are nothing more than memory tasks. (This delay in writing is also exacerbated by the fact that students cannot add new entries while the instructor is reviewing the journal, so the entries naturally fall behind from the beginning of the next cycle.)

Some instructors attempt to overcome these problems by having students submit each journal entry on a separate sheet of paper, subsequently combining them to produce a comprehensive record. While this strategy did avoid the infrequent collection of numerous heavy notebooks, it also introduced other problems to contend with. The greatest flaw with this method of journaling is the lack of continuity in reviewing the entries. The reviewer could not revisit previous entries to see if the student was incorporating the feedback and developing their journaling skills.

TECHNOLOGICAL JOURNALING OPTIONS

In an effort to take advantage of the pedagogical benefits of journaling activities and avoid the problems associated with hardcopy journals, some instructors turned to technological options.

One option was to have students word process their journal entries, thus avoiding the problems of poor handwriting and spelling and grammatical errors. Students would then submit their journals on disks or memory sticks. This method introduced more complications for instructors in the form of technological incompatibilities with students using different platforms or programs to produce their journals. Journals were frequently lost due to system crashes or simply by physically misplacing media.

Some instructors required students to submit journal entries using email. Again, technological problems frequently crept into the assignment. In addition, the individual email journal entries constituted separate reflections and could not be reviewed in the context of the entire evolving journal.

Phipps (2005) suggests the most promising technological solution is the use of course management software to support journaling activities. She points out that this software allows threaded discussions, thus providing comprehensive logs. Since entries are time stamped, it also precludes the last minute rush to complete the entire assignment at one time. Some course management software can also be configured to support private rooms, which can be used by individual students to maintain personal journals within the overall course system.

However, while that electronic option does eliminate some of the "hard copy" problems discussed earlier, it is not without its own difficulties. Many such course management systems require special configurations beyond the technical capabilities of the instructor. Students still do not have the option to create private entries that only they can access.

Finally, most online courses are dismantled at the end of each semester, so the students' journals are destroyed at the end of the term, along with all other material that may reside on the main course platform. In the case of archived courses, the journals will be preserved, but students rarely have access to the archives, so their journals are effectively lost to them.

Therefore, the promise of a technological solution to the problems associated with traditional journaling assignments focuses on a search for the most appropriate technology. Users can choose from a wide range of software programs that support the electronic exchange of ideas, and selecting the best program can be a daunting task. As always, it is critical that instructors clearly define their pedagogical needs prior to selecting the supporting software. Each program will be best suited to particular course parameters, and a poor choice in software may actually inhibit some of the desired instructional activities. For example, this author needed a software program that:

- Was free for faculty and student use
- Was simple and intuitive for users
- Did not require high-end hardware support
- Allowed various levels of security, from private individual postings to wide-open public participation
- Could easily be maintained by the instructor
- Was resident on the provider's server
- Was not embedded in another program, such as a course management system
- Was not a mainstream system that students were likely to already use
- Supported the inclusion of a wide range of media into the posts

These general characteristics suggested the class of software systems designed to support wikis and blogs, and after reviewing numerous such programs, LiveJournal was selected as most closely meeting the requirements previously outlined.

LIVEJOURNAL SUPPORTS E-JOURNALING

The LiveJournal (LJ) program is basically a blogging system. There is a share-ware version that is sufficiently robust for almost any academic or personal use. Additional features available to paid members include additional image uploads, "fast lane" access, and the ability to post by email or phone (livejournal.com). Although LJ has been available since 1999, it is not one of the better known blog systems, so while students may be familiar with the concept of electronic social networking, few will have accounts on this system. This was important in order to be able to separate students' potential social uses of the system from academic assignments. Client inputs are archived on the LJ system so instructors do not need to have access to large storage hardware systems. This intuitive program does not take long to learn. No special knowledge of coding is necessary, yet there are enough point-and-click options built into the system to allow students to customize the look of their own pages. One of the most attractive options of the LJ system is the ability for users to set the security level for each of their posts. This feature allows them to restrict access to their posts to "private" (which only they can read), "custom" (specific designated individuals), "friends" (anyone on their list), and "public" (anyone on the entire web system). LJ also has an email notification system that alerts individuals when there is a new post for them to read. This valuable tool alerts students that the instructor has commented on their posts. However, most instructors will want to disable this feature so they are not constantly inundated with messages about new student posts. Instead they should set regularly scheduled times to review all recent posts.

The following case studies describe methods for using the Live-Journal system to effectively address the problems inherent in journaling activities that use either hard copy or other technological media:

- There are no longer stacks of journal notebooks to carry around, yet each complete journal and the entire class community is maintained, so continuity is guaranteed.

- Handwriting variability and spelling errors are not an issue with a word processed and spell checked document.

- Students and instructors may access the journals at any time for review or comment.

- Instructors gain the flexibility to vary their review schedule so it does not become overwhelming at set points in the semester.

- The nature of the electronic entries also provides the date and time stamp that reinforces timely student entries to avoid the last minute catch-up entries seen in the traditional journals.

- Instructors are able to provide frequent, easily legible and timely feedback. In addition they are able to review earlier journals to see if students have responded to their comments, questions, or suggestions and also to track the overall development of students' progress.

This ability to shape the students' productions throughout the semester also means that students can help shape the direction of the course, as the instructor may modify the assignments in response to student entries. With students in control of the security level for each of their posts:

- They are at liberty to include "private" posts, which they may want to record into their journals but do not wish to share with others.

- They are able to set the security level to allow input from one or more instructors or other individuals as appropriate to the assignment.

- They have the ability to include links to other web sites, images, or sound or video clips that may be relevant to their journal entries.

- Since the entries are archived in a central repository, it is unlikely that individual journals will be lost or destroyed. This central archival system ensures that students may access their own journals after the end of the semester to review them or possibly include them as part of a subsequent portfolio.

Using the LJ system also provides the instructor the opportunity to embed some instruction on the "netiquette" of using a networking system for academic purposes as differentiated from contemporary social purposes. The use of this electronic journaling system may also help prepare students for in-class discussions by affording them the opportunity to consolidate their thoughts and receive feedback on them in a private, structured, and supportive environment prior to being asked to share them with their classmates in open discussions.

Instructors electing to use the LiveJournal system to support journaling activities may still encounter a few roadblocks. Some may be unfamiliar with the use of a social networking system, so it will require some learning on their part. Since they are not in control of the software, the system may occasionally be down for updates. However, these outages are brief, and LJ does post announcements of upcoming downtimes. Because LJ is a shareware program there is no formal support system. However, there is a well-developed help section on the program itself and a very active users group that generally answers any question in a timely manner.

CASE STUDIES

The following cases will provide examples of the ways in which Live-Journal was used to administer journaling assignments in four very different courses. Each case provides a description of the course design, the level of the student, goals of the journal assignment, how that assignment supported the overall pedagogical goals of the course, issues related to the use of LJ, and the grading rubric of the journal assignment. Also presented are the advantages realized by these journaling assignments and some cautions for possible pitfalls.

Before considering specific uses of journals, it is important to review several issues common to all journaling assignments. Regardless of the medium used to support the journaling, the assignment is only as good as the time the instructor invests in the development and administration of the assignment. Prior to the start of the course, the instructor must analyze the goals of the assignment and establish how that one activity supports the overall course goals. The guidelines for each journal entry need to be clearly articulated in terms the student can understand and apply. Grading rubrics need to be clearly specified and obviously contribute to the overall course grade. If students see the journal activity as a noncredit-bearing component of the course or "busywork," they will not treat the assignment seriously. Instructors need to define what they see as their role in the assignment; how actively they participate sets the tone of the journals. In most cases, the instructor is there as a guide and a facilitator, and to probe for deeper reflection, not as an evaluator or a critical reviewer. If students do not feel that their journal content is personal and not subject to criticism, their entries are likely to be superficial and geared toward pacifying the instructor rather than freely expressing their opinions.

Instructors need to realize that, regardless of the medium, journaling activities are writing intensive, and as such they take an inordinate amount of time to administer effectively. If the instructor does not review the journal entries frequently and provide meaningful feedback in a timely manner, the student will persist in bad habits and will not benefit from the activity. It is especially easy for instructors to procrastinate in grading the online journals, as they do not have a physical stack of books sitting in front of them demanding attention. Most instructors need to set aside specific hours each week exclusively for reviewing the journals.

As stated earlier, the goal of most journal assignments is, in some way, to encourage students to reflect more deeply on some specified aspect of their academic experience. They may be asked to reflect on course content, to apply it to their own experiences, or to explore their own motives and self-growth. However, as Spalding and Wilson (2002, 1393) note, "reflection is a mysterious concept to many of the students." Francis (1995, 249) also noted that while reflection is the "way in which teachers construct meanings and knowledge that guide their actions in the classroom . . . reflection is more intellectually challenging than is generally recognized and that too little assistance is provided to (students) to help them observe, think through, reconstruct and deeply understand." While no one method is likely to develop these deep reflective and analytic skills in students, certain key elements have proven to facilitate growth in this area. Instructors must clearly articulate the goals of the journal assignment. They will probably need to devote class time to a discussion of the practice of journaling, or if the course is offered in an online format, they will need to produce written guidelines for the activity. They should also consider providing examples of what they consider to be exemplary journal entries, as many students learn best from following concrete models. The single most effective strategy for improving students' journal writing skills is to provide frequent, timely, and specific personalized feedback to entries. This feedback needs to be nonjudgmental and refer the student back to specific areas of their entries to explain a particular comment, reanalyze some point not considered, apply their comments to other situations, or in some other way elaborate upon and apply their reflections. The instructor needs to remember to review earlier comments to track students' responses to the feedback and to track their growth as journalists. These improvements need to be commented upon to reinforce the student's continued growth.

Case 1: E-Journaling Supplements Traditional Class

The first case involves journaling activities designed to supplement an on-campus course. This class consisted of twenty-five students, most of whom were sophomores that were uncertain of their career choices. They were enrolled in this course to explore potential school-based careers other than teaching. The course consisted of weekly class meetings in which students were introduced to a wide variety of careers, the training and certification requirements for each profession, the actual daily activities of the professionals, the advantages and disadvantages of each career, job forecasts in different regions, and salaries. Students were also introduced to legal aspects related to all school-based professions. Material was presented using in-class lectures and web demonstrations. In addition, guest speakers representing each profession visited the class, and students were assigned a series of readings related to each topic.

Grading for this course consisted of roughly three equal components. First, students were required to produce documents such as curriculum vitae, resumes, cover letters, and portfolios that would later be used in job searchers. Second, they were assigned a series of essay questions related to the actual course content. Finally, they were required to maintain a weekly journal. The journal entries were designed to be a record of the student's personal growth and their reactions to certain careers and issues related to working in schools. Since the journals were clearly personal student reflections, they were not evaluated for accuracy of content. Rather, each entry was scored on timeliness (to ensure reflection on each presentation while it was still relevant and not eclipsed by other materials); depth of reflection; relevance to the material (did they actually reflect on the current topics); and attention to feedback. The instructor also allocated a portion of the grade to spelling and grammar. While some may not wish to evaluate the production elements of the journal because it is a personal reflection, it is also an academic artifact that might later be used as a component of a portfolio, and as such it is appropriate to emphasize the structural elements as well. Journals were reviewed on a weekly basis and students were provided with feedback designed to direct them to earlier entries for deeper reflection and elaboration and also to suggest areas for future development.

All journals were constructed using the LiveJournal (LJ) networking system. The first day of class, students were introduced to the structure of the course as well as to the use of LJ. They were provided with instructor-developed documentation for creating an account on the system and the manner in which they would use it to create and maintain their course journals. As mentioned earlier, the individual creating the posts on LJ is the one who sets the security level, thus determining who may read and respond to the individual posts. In this case, each student in the class created an account specific to this course using the course number and their last name to facilitate searching and sorting by the instructor. Students had the option to use the various templates that LJ supports to personalize their journals. Each week they would create and post a reflective journal entry. Entries could be created off line using a word processor and then cut and pasted into the appropriate spot in LJ, or they could be created directly online with the assistance of the spell checker embedded in the system. Once the text had been created and before the students actually posted the entries, they set the security level to indicate that only the instructor (whom they had listed as a "friend") could access the assigned entries. Students also indicated that they used the "private" listing if they wished to make notes to themselves that they did not want anyone (including the instructor) to read.

It quickly became evident which students in the class had kept some sort of personal journal in the past and those for whom the concept was totally novel. Experienced journalists rapidly caught on to the concept of introspection and recording their reactions to material presented in class. Many wrote lengthy and literary entries that were a pleasure to read and gave the instructor great insight into the student, as well as helping to guide subsequent in-class discussions. Other students clearly struggled with the journals. Not only were they not articulate in the actual entries, but they had no experience in self-reflection or personalizing the course content. In some ways, it is those students who are the most challenging, but also the most rewarding. There is so much room for improvement, and their growth in skills that will be useful to them throughout their lives is so evident. Regardless of the students' facility with journal writing, it quickly became clear that the instructor needed to provide specific questions for students to use as springboards for their reflections. Simply saying "think about what you learned in class and how it applies to you" was not sufficiently directive for many of the students. Specific questions about student's own experience with school personnel in the past, or how an aspect of their personality would interact with the position that had been described, or how they would deal with a student's problem if they were responsible for that student tended to elicit much more detailed answers. Providing the more structured questions initially, and then following up with a more general one to capture reflections that may have occurred to them but not been included elsewhere, yielded the most comprehensive self-reflections.

Case 2: Intern Mentoring

In the second case, e-journals were a central component of an internship program for undergraduate students in placements with school-based professionals. Students in this program worked at their internship site for six hours each week and met on campus one day a week for a group seminar course. Each semester, approximately ten upper-level students take part in this internship opportunity after completing a preparation course on campus the previous semester. Grading for the internship experience is based on an exit evaluation from their site sponsor, an academic product (such as a paper, web site, or video), contributions to the seminar meetings, and daily journal entries for their days at their internship sites.

As all students in the internship course had completed the journaling activity described in Case 1, they were already familiar with both the LJ system and the general format for reflective journals. Again, in this case they were required to reflect on course content presented in seminar meetings and consider how it would apply to them specifically. As mentioned earlier, some students were more facile than others with this approach to personalizing academic content. In addition to responding to course materials, students were assigned readings from Sweitzer and King's (2004) text, *The Successful Internship*. The assigned text has excellent sections reviewing the internships' progress, as well as thought-provoking chapters on issues related to self-discovery and responding to the internship site. Each chapter concludes with questions "for contemplation," which provided excellent structured topics to guide the reflective journal entries. Students also included spontaneous reports of their daily activities at their sites. This was the component that was most difficult for some of the interns. Some maintained excellent logs of exactly how they spent their time, but gave no personal reaction to what they were seeing and doing. Others wrote insightful essays but were weak on the specifics of their actual placement activities. The challenge was to get students to combine these two elements of the reflective journal. Again Sweitzer and King's text was helpful as they discuss the difference between "recording" and "reflecting." They proceed to outline techniques for integrating the two tasks. Some of the suggested techniques that the interns found most useful were dividing their journals into five categories: (1) knowledge, (2) skills, (3) personal growth, (4) career development, and (5) civic development (2004, 32). Sweitzer and King point out that a reflective journal is a place to help turn the internship experience into a learning experience by stopping to recall the events of the day and then analyze and process them. One way they suggest accomplishing this is the "dual entry," where students record what happened and their reactions to it. They then relate it to relevant concepts from class or readings. Students also like the "critical incident journals" (34), in which they identify one specific incident from the week and write about it in some depth.

Another technique for integrating the daily log with the reflective component is a modification of Weinstein's (1981) "three column processing" (in Sweitzer and King 2004, 34). Following this approach, students record those things they actually saw or heard (they may elect to apply this approach to only a select few incidents per week). Next, they review the list and try to remember what they were thinking when the action occurred. They then recall how they were feeling when the action took place. Finally, they reflect on what they learned from the incident and what they could have done differently. Thus, the internship journals provided a structured log of the student's daily activities and also chronicled their growth as professionals. The LJ system is flexible enough to allow participants to select any of these methods, or to switch among them from entry to entry as the situation dictates. The challenge for the instructor is to suggest and model the optimal format as the students progress through the hierarchy of involvement, understanding, and self-awareness.

Once again, it was the students who created the LJ posts, and they were the ones who determined who could read and respond to their posts. Students were encouraged to create "private" entries for reflections that they felt were personally meaningful parts of the internship experience, but that they did not wish to share with anyone else. Some of their journal entries would be restricted to viewing by the class instructor. These entries allowed the student to raise concerns they might have that related to their site supervisor but that they did not want to share with that individual. Additionally, these posts to the campus supervisor could cover topics related only to academic policy or future plans unrelated to the worksite supervisor. This ability to restrict access to posts also allowed interns to post entries that only the site supervisor could access. This was useful when the student needed to discuss work issues with the site supervisor without violating confidentiality guidelines. For this course, most of the posts were designated to be accessed by both the campus supervisor and the site sponsor. This allowed for a timely integration of feedback from both supervisors and ensured that all concerned were reviewing the student's progress and could monitor the associated growth in the domain. It was also a valuable tool for appraising both supervisors of what the student was seeing at work and how they were relating it to the academic content. All parties could ensure that there was no conflict in the feedback given, and that the student was applying academic content appropriately.

Using the LJ system to maintain these journals also allowed students the opportunity to include other artifacts into their journal entries. For example, many entries would contain active links to web sites the student had found and that were directly relevant to their academic and/or practical experience. They also were able to include scanned images of documents they may be working with at the site, thus creating a valuable archive for themselves. Some of the students included video clips of themselves working at their internship sites, and some added audio clips of interviews with students with whom they were working.

In this way, the internship journals became valuable documents of the students' growth and self-reflection and provided a dynamic medium for mentoring by two physically separated supervisors. As the journals would be archived by the LJ system, they would be readily available to students who could elect to use them at a later time as part of their professional portfolios or application materials.

In a few instances, students who had completed an internship while in residence on campus elected to engage in a later one at a remote site. In these situations, the use of the e-journals (following the format outlined above) became an even more critical component of their internship because it allowed for a fluid integration of feedback, supervision, and mentoring by the campus supervisor and the site supervisor. The use of the LJ system of e-journaling enabled desirable remote internship experiences that had previously been impractical due to the difficulties of coordinating activities of students and supervisors who were never in actual physical proximity.

Case 3: Constructivist Community Building

The third case employs a very different paradigm than that described in the first two cases. In this instance, the e-journals are used as a component of a totally online graduate-level course. As students enrolled in the course never physically meet, it can be difficult to build a sense of community to allow students to share their ideas, reflections, and opinions in an open and constructive manner. LJ provided the "virtual community" to accomplish those goals.

The first two cases describe private journals which individual students create and maintain in response to questions given in class by the instructor. The student creating the journal sets the security level and determines who can access their work. However in this case, the journals take on a group aspect, and the instructor sets the security level with this structure. While the journals are still used as a platform for students to reflect on topics and record their intellectual growth over the course of a semester, they are also an avenue to encourage group interaction.

This course consisted of fifteen psychology graduate students who were assigned a weekly set of readings; the instructor posted related questions to the LJ site. Students created LJ accounts according to the guidelines distributed by the instructor. Subsequently, the instructor created a "custom group" to include only those students enrolled in the course. Each week, the instructor posted the reflection question and set the security so that all the students in the class could read and respond to it. In this way, students were also able to access the posts of their classmates, as they were all included in the initial security level set by the instructor. Students were permitted to maintain some "private" posts if they wished, but all were required to post to the group and respond to group inputs.

As previously mentioned, it is critical that the journaling activity be fully integrated into the course requirements and the overall grading rubrics. In this course, the discussions constituted approximately one-third of the student's grade. The questions for this activity consisted of student reactions to the assigned readings as well as their descriptions of possible applications of the concepts to their lives and careers. As such, it was not possible to evaluate the student responses for accuracy, so the instructor had to establish other criteria. As a result, each weekly discussion contained several graded components. First, students received a grade for the completeness of their response to the question posed by the instructor: did their answer address all components of the question; did it demonstrate that they had read and understood the assigned readings; and, did it include references to related scholarly material they had located themselves. Second, students were required to respond to at least three of their peer's postings. The instructor graded these responses on the depth of the students' input and their ability to pose probing questions in response to the original posting. This posting–response model encouraged a great deal of class integration. Students learned from each other and also learned how to provide constructive feedback and criticism where appropriate in order to encourage their peers to elaborate or reflect more deeply on their initial post.

This exercise proved to be successful in facilitating the desired sense of community and allowing students to reflect on each other's work. However, creating this constructivist learning environment did pose some significant challenges for the instructor. First, the instructor needs to clearly establish her role in the activity. This can be a delicate balance. If the instructor is too active in discussions, it may inhibit student responses; they tend to wait for the instructor to set the tone and direct the flow of the discussion. However, if the instructor does not have a visible presence in the discussion, it may flow off track or take on negative tones. The balance that seems to work best is for the instructor to set the initial question, then establish the dates by which initial posts and responses should be made. While students are engaged in those activities, the instructor simply monitors the discussion and, if necessary, shapes individual student's entries if they are not appropriate to the discussion forum. When each weekly discussion is complete, the instructor makes general comments to the group and specific, usually private, comments to individuals, to wrap up the activity. This format clearly demonstrates that the instructor is observing and facilitating the discussion, but that the students are in control of constructing their own relevance of the topic.

Another challenge for the instructor is in setting the initial question. If the question is too controversial, especially early in the semester when the group identity has not been formed, students may be hesitant to openly express their opinions. However, if the question is too banal and the answer is obvious, there is little for students to comment on or probe deeper into. The somewhat controversial ideal question includes some elements that are open to interpretation, and allows students to apply their previous learning and personalize their response.

It is also possible to expand the previously described method to include other groups in specific discussions. For example, several of the weekly discussion topics were excellent candidates for cross-cultural comparisons. For those topics, the instructor posed the question based on the assigned reading as usual. However, for those weeks she set the security level to include students enrolled in the primary class as well as those enrolled in a parallel course being offered by a colleague in a different country. In this way, the discussion was still restricted to students enrolled in those courses, but all of them could post comments, read their peers' posts, and respond to them. This activity provided a secure and supportive environment for students to share ideas and interact with contemporary students with a markedly diverse cultural viewpoint.

It was also possible for the instructor to open some discussions to the entire digital community if the topic would benefit from input from a wider audience. Of course, instructors must weigh whether the benefits of the broader participation will offset the requirement for tighter monitoring of message traffic. When the instructor sets the security for the weekly post as "public," it allows anyone on the Internet to read and respond to the posts for that week only. All the previous posts were closed, and subsequent topics could once again become restricted to class members only. When the posts were public, the discussion topic functioned as a blog or wiki with open input possible.

By varying the security level of the posts, the instructor was able to provide a broader forum for discussion where appropriate but still retain a sense of class privacy when necessary. Varying the access level to the discussions also introduced students to the concept of writing for specific audiences and modifying their discussions appropriately.

Case 4: Interdisciplinary Integration

The final case involves the use of e-journals to facilitate sharing of work for students in linked courses. In this case, the students were approximately twenty-five members of a freshman learning community who were all enrolled in four foundation courses taught by four different instructors. Students, instructors, and teaching assistants all created accounts on LJ using a naming structure that identified them as members of the cohort group.

Throughout the semester, several different types of journals were created by the students and instructors. Students each created a personal journal in which they entered reflections about their weekly activities and their transition to college. Because the students created these journals, they were the ones who set the security level, following guidelines set by the coordinating instructor. Some posts were sensitive and "private," so only the student could read it and look back on it as the semester progressed. Other journal entries were for class assignments and needed to be accessible to the appropriate instructor(s) and classmates. As previously mentioned, some students were intuitively more attuned to this activity, and others needed specific coaching and suggested topics for reflection.

In addition to these personal reflection journals, instructors would create questions that linked content from two or more of their courses. The instructor who posted the question was responsible for setting the security level so that all the students could read and respond to the question, as well as view their peers' comments. This was an excellent way to continue discussions begun in one class and relate it to content subsequently presented in another class. Without the medium of LJ, it would have been difficult for instructors to assign review questions related to multiple classes and have all instructors involved able to read and respond to the posts simultaneously. This ability to create interdisciplinary connections and receive feedback from classmates and instructors forged the cohort group into a strong community of learners who were able to see the relationship between what otherwise might have been disjoint academic courses.

One additional advantage of using the LJ system to support the activities of the learning community was the ability of students to personalize their own journal space. This flexibility allowed students to include personal pictures, which greatly reduced the time needed to associate names with faces in the group. Students in this cohort group also took advantage of some of the social networking aspects of the LJ system by using it to contact others in the class for nonacademic issues. Again, the advantages of the security levels were that these off-task activities could be conducted privately and not intrude on the actual functions of the class.

CONCLUSION

While the goals and advantages of journaling activities have stood the test of time, the mechanisms by which they were traditionally delivered were cumbersome to both the instructor and the student. The application of emerging social networking technologies, such as LJ, to these traditional academic functions may help to alleviate some of the problems previously associated with these assignments. Of course, there is considerable temptation to incorporate novel technology in otherwise conventional courses simply because it is novel, and instructors must avoid this trap. As always, pedagogical purpose must remain the primary consideration in selecting the type of media used if the integrity of the activities themselves is to be maintained.

REFERENCES

Francis, Dawn. 1995. The reflective journal: A window to preservice teachers' practical knowledge. *Teaching and Teacher Education, 11*(3): 229–241.

Phipps, Jonnie Jill. 2005. E-journaling: Achieving interactive education online. *Educause Quarterly, 28*(1): 62–65.

Spalding, Elizabeth, and Angene Wilson. 2002. Demystifying reflection: A study of pedagogical strategies that encourage reflective journal writing. *The Teachers College Record, 104*(7): 1393–1421.

Sweitzer, Frederick H., and Mary A. King. 2004. *The successful internship: Personal, professional and civic development.* Belmont, CA: Brooks/Cole.

Weinstein, Gerald. 1981. Self-science education. In Jane Fried (Ed.), *New direction for student services: Education for student development.* San Francisco: Jossey Bass.

Online Teaching

The Joys of Joining the Discussion

M. Louise Ripley
York University

Workers today are expected to be well-versed in online communication and computers; to be quick and continual learners; to know how to juggle responsibilities and manage time; to be skilled in problem solving and critical thinking; to excel in teamwork and interpersonal relationships; to be attentive to detail and able to comprehend the larger picture; to be adaptable, creative, enthusiastic, flexible, persistent, self- confident; and to possess an ability to work under pressure. All these abilities can be developed and honed in courses with good online discussion groups; and online courses, although daunting at first, can bring new life to your teaching, especially if you have been working with the same courses for a long time, as I had been. Best of all and most surprising, I found that my online discussion groups provided far more and far better class discussions than I had been experiencing in my too-large, on-campus classrooms, provided I joined the discussion. All it took was the realization that I had three main obligations, and that meeting those obligations involved sorting my work into three main duties.

THREE MAIN OBLIGATIONS

Online course work needs to be meaningful and technically easy to do. To accomplish this, the online professor has three obligations: to ensure that everything online is there for an academic reason, to ensure that online students are aware of what is coming from the first day of classes, and to ensure that everything used online works properly. All of this enhances the learning experience for everyone involved much more if the professor joins the students in the discussion group.

After twenty years of teaching Introductory Marketing in the classroom, I have now taught it exclusively online for seven years. The course contains Learning Units, each with "waving hand exercises," accompanied by an animated graphic of a hand waving to be called on. Students answer these questions in an online discussion group and then comment on each others' answers. Even the simplest task can be academic content related. My first exercise asks students to test the system (Figure 1).

Your second obligation is to ensure that students are informed as much as possible as soon as they begin the course. Online courses are difficult enough for students, given the greater need for self-discipline, and anything you can do to make things easier for them will be appreciated. Happy, relaxed students are more willing to talk about the subject matter in the discussion group rather than their gripes about how the course wasn't what they expected it to be, and they tend to give higher ratings on course evaluation forms. My student evaluations, which were high already, actually rose when I started to teach online. However, if you were just handed the assignment to teach a new online course in two weeks, do not panic; it can and has been done. Technology can help with such things as listing all links but making only two weeks' links active at a time, giving the appearance that everything is there, while you hurry to catch up. It is not ideal, but the reality is that these kinds of assignments do occur.

Your third obligation is to ensure that everything works and works properly. Too many professors are lured into online teaching with promises of easy work or support that does not materialize. Be aware that online teaching is not easy, but that it is not beyond your reach either. To do it well, however, you will require certain basics. You must have a rudimentary knowledge of how things work on the Web, a thorough understanding of how things work within your own teaching web site, and the email address of good help for when things go wrong. You need an advanced computer, with a large high-resolution monitor, an ergonomic keyboard and chair (you will spend a lot of time at your computer), a high-speed Internet connection, and the proper software if you plan to design your own web material. You also need the help of people with skill sets that you may lack the time, desire, or necessity to learn. Most of all, you need a platform on which to organize your discussion group. There are various ones out there, including Moodle, WebCT, Blackboard, or even an email listserv if your school cannot afford to subscribe to a platform. The discussion group is where the majority of the work of a good online course takes place, and it has been said that the role of the professor in an online course is not only teacher but also facilitator, meeting chair, organizer, and host.

EXERCISE:
Testing the
System 1.1

Practice sending a message. Tell us
something you like or dislike about
marketing: perhaps a favourite ad
and why you like it.

Figure 1. Exercise: Testing the system

Organizational Duties: Set the Stage

It is the professor's duty to establish course requirements, objectives, and structure; to set schedules, activities, and timetables; to establish rules, decision-making norms, and expectations; to demonstrate intellectual leadership, academic relevance, and helpful direction in managing interactions; and to make changes as necessary in technical aspects of the course, the direction of its discussion, or sometimes its content.

It helps to remember that online teaching is quintessentially different from on-campus teaching. Students expect more flexibility, and professors expect students to be more self-motivated. You need to make your expectations even clearer than in an on-campus course, right from the start, and it can help to ask students what their expectations are. Undergraduate students generally do not like freewheeling courses where they are expected to just find their own way. My course outline tells students that much of the responsibility for learning in an online course rests with them and that I provide a lot of flexibility, but it also warns them of the need for self-discipline in online courses and provides an optional highly structured format for those who crave it. Teaching and learning materials are different. The student who anticipates twelve lectures ready to print from the screen and the professor who plans to deliver an online course merely by taping classroom lectures and streaming them on the Web are not making use of the myriad of opportunities that the Internet and online communication provide. In addition to such things as iPod connections, links to other web sites, the huge potential for stationary and animated graphics, the ability to include sound and motion additions to your materials, and much more, there is also, top among these, the discussion group, with the professor as an active participant.

I noticed better discussions online than I did in the classroom. Online students tend to be more willing to "speak up," perhaps finding it easier to put fingers to keyboard than to raise a hand in a room full of peers who can see them. This is partly due to increasingly large class sizes in most of our schools as budgets are slashed. It is particularly true for many students who, due to upbringing related to gender, class, or culture, have not previously felt empowered to speak in the classroom. I get to know my students better online; they will share personal stories in a relatively anonymous web discussion group that I never hear in a classroom.

You need to set expectations early in the course: how much and how frequently students should contribute to the discussion group, how quickly you will respond when they have a question, and how they can reach you. Students expect you to be more available for them. This does not mean you must be there every minute, and styles will differ. Some professors prefer to keep a more formal presence, offering specific online office hours. Others prefer to check into the course site regularly, to deal with questions as they arise, and to facilitate discussion as it proceeds. Most formats are acceptable to students; they just need to know what your format is and for you to be reasonably consistent. This does not mean you have to spend fifteen hours a day, seven days a week working with the discussion group, although that can easily happen if you do not set boundaries. It is what I spent the most time on in the first online course I taught. Today, with more experience, I still spend much more time with my online students than I ever do in on-campus courses, but there are tradeoffs. I no longer sit alone in my office, committed to "office hours" that no student can utilize. With students working more to fund an increasingly costly education, they are unable to come to talk with me, but they can always find time to ask their question in the electronic discussion group. Sometimes the person who answers their question is me, but frequently it is another student. Generally, online students tend to be supportive of each other. This is an important aspect of online discussion groups for students, as in their careers they will need to be experienced in and feel comfortable with seeking and giving information electronically with peers whom they may never meet. Also, I thoroughly enjoy my online discussion groups. I frequently log in on an evening or on the weekend just to see what interesting talk is going on. My students are bright, talented, interesting, and funny; and I enjoy our conversations about marketing and their experiences with the course. I get to know them well enough to write highly successful letters of recommendation for jobs and graduate schools.

While large class sizes frequently prohibit giving marks for discussion, in an online course, you must give credit if you want students to "talk." This means you will need a method of keeping track of student participation. Most host platforms provide some method of tracking, and even in a simple listserv you can at least do a manual count. In this respect, online is superior to on-campus discussion, providing names in print attached to the comments. Ideally, marks should relate to content as well as quantity, but in reality you may not have the resources to do this and a count of postings seems acceptable to most students.

There are a variety of ways to organize online discussion groups. Some professors divide the class into sections, each with its own group. I first used one large group where all the students and I were signed up to a listserv, which sent messages into each person's email inbox. However, in a course with 10 units, 20 questions each, and 100 students, the effort to sort through 20,000+ emails soon became overwhelming. Eventually I moved to WebCT, a platform for teaching online that makes organizing discussion much easier, and we will soon be moving to Moodle. I still keep the entire class together, because as an active participant I prefer to work with just one group. I create a separate topic for each Learning Unit, and a number of additional discussion topics related to tests, assignments, general student questions, group projects, and notes from the professor. In this last one, I post the kinds of things I would often say at the start of an on-campus class: reminders of assignments due, a notice that a course topic was covered in today's newspaper, a clarification if too many people misunderstood an item in a recent discussion, even wishes for a happy holiday that is coming up.

One of your responsibilities as moderator is to keep the discussion group relatively clutter free. This may entail closing down topics after a certain date or sending them to an archives file; this also encourages students to work in a timely manner. One advantage to teaching with online material is that you can immediately correct things that do not work, are in error, or need to be updated. Use these situations as learning opportunities; it is empowering for a student to be able to point out to the professor more current practices used at their place of work, which you can then add to the Learning Unit.

Social Duties: Create the Environment

Your social duties are to create an environment for learning and a sense of community. So many large universities and colleges are already difficult places for students to find community, especially when most students commute. The potential for alienation in distance education is far greater; students may never see each other face-to-face. You can create a sense of community through a number of relatively easy measures.

Send students a welcoming email a few days before classes start, explaining how the course is run, and encouraging them to get started early and to enjoy the learning experiences offered. Tell them something about yourself. I have a "personal" page on my web site. Voluntary posting of student pictures on the web site helps students to get to know each other. Find something of value in each early posting, no matter what the student has said, to encourage everyone to write more. From the start, reassure students who are worried about the course, the Web, or the technology, and keep doing this as new students arrive. Show students that their comments are valued. Do not simply say, "You're right, Jim." Tell Jim, and the class, exactly what it was about his posting that was good: "Jim, I like your example of the demographic factor in your comment about segmenting the market for cell phones; age clearly makes a difference in the kinds of ads that will appeal to different users." Ask for personal experiences whenever possible when asking them to give examples of practice linked to theory. Use students' names prolifically when responding to their postings. Pick up on personal traits and stories that they have used in answering the exercises and refer back to these. "Mary, this posting reminds me of Qiang's story about buying the camera last Christmas . . ." Nothing gets people's attention faster than the use of their own name!

Remember that how you work together in a learning environment is as important as what gets done. You want students to work with the course material to ensure they learn the terminology and theory of the field, but it is equally important, particularly in an online course, that students feel comfortable exploring ideas and believe that their contribution is valued.

As the professor, you set the tone for discussion from the first day, not only assuring students that their input is valued, but also assuring them that strong deviations from norms will not be encouraged. Thus, if early in the course, you find someone dominating the discussion, being rude to other students or yourself, or consistently responding in a negative way, you need to show leadership and quickly bring things back under control. Ideally, you have already formally dealt with the issue of etiquette (often referred to as "netiquette" in online work) in the syllabus, to which you can privately refer the offending student. If that does not work, you may post a public request for the behavior to cease. If this fails, find out what resources are available at your school to handle disruptive students, from intervention by a department chair or dean to having the student dropped from the course or even the school. On a positive note, in my experience such behavior is rare.

As teachers, we need to know how our students are doing, what they find difficult or too easy, what motivates and encourages them, and what distresses and slows them down. You can learn all of this by participating with them in the discussion group. You may also learn more about your subject. In an active discussion group with properly designed questions, online students tend to bring an amazing amount of current knowledge and practice from their own work and experience that greatly enhances the learning experience for other students and the professor.

Intellectual Duties: Act as Facilitator

Your primary role is always that of a facilitator of learning. You set the tone for the course and the discussion; you ensure things are done in a way that encourages learning. You make sure that what the students were promised in the course syllabus happens. And your presence online enables your students to see your own curiosity and excitement about your chosen field. State your goals and objectives clearly in your syllabus. If your course does not meet a student's needs, students have a right to know that before they decide to stay enrolled. It also is helpful if you receive a complaint about the course not meeting expectations, to be able to show that you had clearly and in a timely manner informed students of both content and structure.

Do not be afraid to use terminology and theory right from the start. I begin on the first day of classes using the terminology of the field in my postings. By the time students encounter the words in the textbook, they have already been exposed to them. Refer back to the text frequently; keep luring them into the theory. Learn to read between the lines of students' responses, to pull out things that are important, linked directly to theory, but which they may not recognize they have included. Keep telling the ones whose postings relate to theory how worthwhile it is to do this, and soon others will do it too: "I love Indira's example here of positioning in her story about how the store where she works changed its emphasis on what it was going to sell next year."

Part of your job as moderator is to keep the discussion on track. It can be useful to occasionally let it wander because wondrous learning opportunities can come out of unplanned diversions, but you must ensure that it does not go so far astray that students become bored, puzzled, or angry. I provide a special topic labeled "General Course Questions and Comments" where students can log on, knowing that the talk will be less structured and that they can bring up a subject that is only tangentially related to the course but of interest to them. Students frequently send messages to this topic, telling us about newspaper articles, something they have seen on television, or something that happened to them in a store or on the job. Students know that things discussed in this topic will not be on the exam, leaving them free to discuss things there for the pure joy of learning, but we try to keep the Learning Unit topics on track.

Another of your intellectual duties is to summarize and synthesize postings and their relation to other course material, and eventually to lead your students to do this. You need to regularly summarize discussion for example, at the end of a unit or at the end of a particularly long or complicated exchange, to provide a unifying overview: "Now that we have covered the basic elements of marketing, we can see from your answers that three of the most important terms to remember are target market, customer need, and segmentation." You also need to encourage students to look up from the details they are studying and get a glimpse of the bigger picture: "How do these three factors from the first unit relate to the need for positioning a product in the market, which we studied in the second unit?"

You must know when to ask the right questions. Part of your responsibility as moderator is to encourage students to look more deeply at their sometimes superficial answers to get them to question their own assumptions and biases. You need to do this in a way that does not leave students feeling that they have "failed" in their answers, and in a way that will encourage all students to consider their answers carefully. One of the most common problems I face in teaching Introductory Marketing is that everyone has seen marketing since they were old enough to be put in a stroller and wheeled through the shopping mall. Students often start with easy, generalized answers that anyone could write without reading a marketing textbook. My job at this point is to draw them back into the text, the web site, the theory and terminology, but to do it without making them feel inadequate. I use a lot of phrases like, "That's a great response! Now, can we put it into marketing terminology?" Or, "Good! Now—into which of the eight cells of Hunt's Three Dichotomies Model would you throw that question?"

One of the most helpful things I learned about moderating discussion groups is that if you do something from the start, no student feels criticized if you do it in response to their particular posting. However, if you have been blithely and generously saying, "Great response!" to everything posted, and then suddenly you seem to dare to ask, "Where is the theory that backs this up?" a student may rightfully feel anxious. So, from the start, you need to find that delicate balance between "supportive" and "pushing for more" in your responses to students' postings. Do not be afraid to step in and urge students to consider more detailed answers, to question their assumptions and biases, to ask them to reconsider answers that you know to be wrong or insufficient. It is all part of your role as educational facilitator. You also need to be sure not to post your own opinion or understanding of an issue too quickly. Tell students that you will provide your answer later in the course and keep the field open for them.

You cannot do any of this if you have relegated supervision of the discussion group to a teaching assistant or if you just let students converse with each other. You could, of course, just list these summaries at the end of a Learning Unit, but students will understand them more fully if they have worked them out through discussion with both their peers and you. Besides, this is the most exciting part of teaching! It also encourages further talk and learning, as students see the application of their thoughts and experiences to the material being studied, and it leads to creative and critical thinking.

IMPROVING THE COURSE BY JOINING THE DISCUSSION GROUP: AN EXAMPLE

I first prepared the "waving hand exercises" without full realization of how they would work. It was not until I took part in the discussion group with my students that I realized the problem with questions like, "In what range of colors was Henry Ford's first car offered?" The simple factual answer "black" grew rather irritating when it arrived in 100 emails. I knew what I wanted students to do. I wanted them to say, "Black, because that was all that Ford produced, but there was no other car so people had to buy his black cars." However, students will usually answer the question you ask, and they answered, "Black." So I soon changed the question (Figure 2).

They now engage in interesting discussions about the exact issue I wanted them to consider. This not only provides more interesting answers, it makes for more learner-centered exercises. I would not have discovered this had I not been an active participant in the discussion group, receiving all those messages saying simply, "black." I also find that with me as an active member, students feel freer to (politely) write and tell me when things do not work well, or are not interesting to do, or might be im-

<table>
<tr><td>EXERCISE:
Henry Ford
1.7</td><td>Henry Ford said of his early automobile that people could have it in any colour they wanted as long as it was black. Why was Ford able to make this statement?</td></tr>
</table>

Figure 2. Exercise: Henry Ford

proved in the course exercises, and I can make changes. We develop a closeness in the discussions that enhances everything about teaching a course.

EXPERIENTIAL LEARNING: AN EXAMPLE OF THE "WAVING HAND EXERCISES"

I encourage students to refer to their own experience when answering questions, and frequently I give them specific tasks to acquire experiences in what I refer to as one of the largest laboratories they will ever find in a course: the "real world" of shopping and buying. Figures 3 and 4 deal with an exercise using Peter Drucker's Five Questions to ask when analyzing your business.

A frequent concern of online teachers is whether we are "teaching" or "facilitating." We need to remember that we teach in other ways than when we stand before a seated group of students busily taking down our every word. Often the best teaching is done when students experience first hand the problems faced in the field and wrestle with possible answers. Experiential education is a major key to better teaching, and it can easily be done in online teaching.

CONCLUSION

My greatest concern in converting an on-campus course to an online course was that I would miss being with my students in the classroom. I worried about them not being able to "see" me; I was unsure how well my web pages would "substitute" for my actual presence. I worried about my ability to read a classroom, to know by the looks on their faces and the subtle (and sometimes not-so-subtle) noises and shifting in seats whether the material was holding their interest. Most of all, I worried that I would no longer get to know my students. Even in large classes, I have always made

EXERCISE:
Lab Coffee
2.2

Peter Drucker's Five Questions - Read through the Coffee Exercise below, then go to a coffee shop near you, order something and sit for a while and watch the coffee drinkers.. Then complete the Coffee Exercise and Post to the Discussion Group.

Figure 3. Exercise: Lab coffee.

1. What is our business? To figure out what your mission is and how you will best meet your customer's needs, you first need to know what business you're in: who you are, what you do well, what is important to you. What business is this coffee shop in? .... (the exercise continues with all 5

Figure 4. What is our business?

it a priority to get to know as many students as possible, not only by name, but by their stories, their jobs, their problems, and their families, all the things that students bring to a classroom that make it come alive. I am a great believer in the power of discussion to facilitate learning, even in large classrooms. I rely for the excitement and fun in my marketing classes on having students who know something about the marketplace, as consumers, as viewers of television, as readers of magazines, as people who live and work in a world that is permeated by marketing, and on their willingness to share their stories in the classroom. I worried that I would miss all this in an online course where I would never "see" my students and where, I feared, we would never get to talk to each other.

I learned quickly that it would be the discussion group that would keep me from losing all the things I valued most in a classroom. Properly structured, an online course discussion group, in addition to enhancing the life-long learning skills of your students, also can provide just as much opportunity to get to know your students and to get a sense of your classroom as does a traditional on-campus course, sometimes more, but you must be there with them online. Furthermore, I think I can promise you that you will enjoy being there with them.

Using Electronic Portfolios to Foster Communication in K–12 Classrooms

Elizabeth Meyer, Anne Wade, Vanitha Pillay,
Einat Idan, and Philip C. Abrami

Concordia University

An electronic portfolio (EP) is a digital container capable of storing visual and auditory content including text, images, video, and sound. EPs may also be learning tools not only because they organize content, but also because they are designed to support a variety of pedagogical processes, including reflecting on one's own learning and providing feedback to peers to stimulate their own reflections (Abrami and Barrett 2005; Wade, Abrami, and Sclater 2005). This reflection process is a key element in students' learning, and effective communication between students is an important part of this process. EPs have three broad purposes: assessment, presentation, and process. For assessment purposes, EPs can be used as examples of students' authentic activity and are especially useful for formative purposes, showing progress over time; whereas presentation portfolios are used to represent students' most important work. This article focuses on the process piece of EPs, as this is central to the theme of student engagement addressed in this book.

EPs may be designed as *process (or learning) portfolios* supporting how users learn through embedded structures and strategies. A process EP is a purposeful collection of student work that tells the story of a student's effort, progress, and/or achievement in one or more areas (Arter and Spandel 1992; MacIsaac and Jackson 1994). Process portfolios are personal learning management tools. They are meant to encourage individual improvement, personal growth and development, and a commitment to lifelong learning. The authors are especially interested in the use of EPs as process portfolios to support learning.

Process EPs are gaining in popularity for multiple reasons. They provide multimedia display and assessment possibilities for school and work contexts, allowing the use of a variety of tools to demonstrate and develop understanding—especially advantageous for at-risk children whose competencies may be better reflected through these authentic tasks. At the same time, by engaging these learners, their deficiencies in core competencies such as reading, writing, and general learning skills may be overcome. Process EPs may scaffold attempts at knowledge construction by supporting reflection, refinement, conferencing, and other processes of self-regulation, important skills for lifelong learning and learning how to learn. They are superior for cataloging and organizing learning materials, better illustrating the process of learner development. Many EPs are web-based, so they can also provide remote access encouraging anywhere, anytime learning and easier input from peers, parents, and educators, letting them provide feedback through a single electronic container. In this regard, they may be used to foster communication between teacher–student, student–student, and child–parent throughout the learning process.

ePEARL: AN EXAMPLE OF AN e-PORTFOLIO TOOL

The Centre for the Study of Learning and Performance (CSLP) based at Concordia University in Montreal in collaboration with their partner LEARN,[1] developed a web-based, student-centered electronic portfolio software named ePEARL, electronic Portfolio Encouraging Active Reflective Learning (http://grover.concordia.ca/epearl/en/), that is designed to develop self-regulated learning (Zimmerman 1989, 2000; Zimmerman and Tsikalas 2005) and improved communication skills in students. Three levels of ePEARL have been designed for use in early elementary (level 1), late elementary (level 2), and secondary schools (level 3). With ePEARL, students can: personalize their portfolio; set long- and short-term goals; create new work through use of a text editor and audio recorder, or link to digital files created outside of the tool; reflect on work; share work with classmates; provide and receive feedback from teachers, peers, and parents; edit work; save work under multiple versions; and send work to a presentation portfolio. The artifacts index page offers students and teachers an easy way to store, organize, and track the progress of assignments (Figure 1).

The ePEARL software is designed to promote a student's self-regulated process of learning. The software prompts the creation of general learning goals for a term or year or for a specific artifact (G); reflection on work in progress or completed work (R); and peer, parent, and teacher feedback (C) on the portfolio or on a specific artifact. Teachers may also provide feedback on the student's goal setting and reflection that has occurred within the portfolio. The ePEARL environment guides students through the creation process. The software also offers the ability to attach work completed using other software (A), so it can accommodate any kind of digital work a student creates, including podcasts, videos, PowerPoint files, or scanned images or photographs of paper-based work.

Before work is created, students are encouraged to set their goals for the assignment and may attach learning logs, evaluation rubrics, and study plans to keep track of their learning process as it takes place. After the creation of work, sharing with peers or teachers is encouraged so students may solicit feedback on drafts of work. Students may also reflect on their performance and strategies to adjust their goals for the next assignment. Sharing with peers is prompted in the reflection screen.

Once students have completed a version of an assignment, they are asked if they would like to share this piece with classmates to obtain feed-

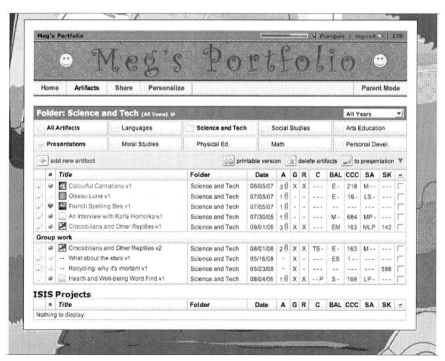

Figure 1. Artifacts index page — Science and technology folder

back (Figure 2). Teachers have automatic access to view and enter feed-back in all of their students' ePEARLs.

The "Presentations" folder within ePEARL is where students collect selected important artifacts. This provides a cumulative area where arti-facts are carried over to the next level of the software and acts as an archive of stored work during a student's educational career. The selection pro-cess allows students to reflect on why they feel an artifact belongs in their "Presentations" folder, its relationship to other work, and on their own ad-vancements.

FACILITATING COMMUNICATION THROUGH DESIGN

An EP, by definition, is a way to externalize an individual's thought pro-cesses and progressions. When beginning an ePEARL entry, the student is walked through a creation process that models a certain level of expert practice, including forethought, performance, and self-reflection. Some cognitive scaffolding is made explicit at this stage, enabling students to easily address aspects or initiate practices that they may not realize are necessary or beneficial to their learning process, such as reflecting on both the final content *and* the process. As these skills and practices are adopted

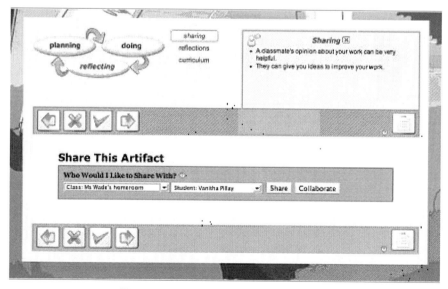

Figure 2. Reflection screen — Sharing

and internalized by the learner, this guided step-by-step scaffolding can be skipped. The ePEARL software is designed to give the individual student a view of his or her own progress. By the end of the guided process, and possibly after several drafts, the learner is ready to make a selection of work he or she would like to display. Reflection is also actively encouraged at this point by urging learners to consider the merits of the final work, the process, and the contribution made to the student's awareness of himself or herself as a learner.

Particular features in ePEARL are intended to facilitate communication between individuals. The software allows students in the same class or school or across schools to comment on work in each other's portfolios. Students receiving the comments are encouraged to revise their work, incorporating those comments they feel are helpful. Teachers are also able to comment on goals and strategies selected by the student and thus help monitor and adjust individual student progress and understanding. Apart from facilitating the communication between teacher and students, this feature also pedagogically supports the teacher by clearly identifying where a teacher's comment may be inserted and can provide the greatest help. The design of ePEARL was focused on encouraging scholastic communication between students and their parents. Given that the learning environment is not limited to the classroom, practices at home are central to a student's academic success. The ePEARL software encourages parents to participate in their child's learning process by commenting on individual work as well as on the portfolio as a whole.

COMMUNICATING EFFECTIVELY THROUGH ePEARL'S FEEDBACK FEATURE

The feedback feature in ePEARL facilitates ongoing communication between students, teachers, and parents through the learning process. However, feedback is only effective if offered consistently and constructively. From our experience and observations, quality feedback is not easy to provide and has to be supported and facilitated through the software with examples and prompts for teachers, students, and parents to be used successfully.

It is sometimes difficult for teachers to give comments relevant to the students' goals, work, or reflections. We have identified three important key factors to keep in mind when giving a student feedback. First, the teacher is setting an example, as well as a standard, for his or her classroom. Students will learn from their teacher how to provide constructive feedback. Teachers can ask themselves several questions when providing comments or feedback on students' portfolios. For example: "Did the student reach his or her goal?" "Why or why not?" "How effective are his or her strategies?" "Are these strategies well linked to the task goal?" Second, teachers can refer students to prompts used in the class (such as "two to glow and one to grow" or "Have you thought about ..."), resources available in the classroom (such as posters or handouts), or to other students that can help them. Third, users should refer to resources available within the software. The ePEARL software offers built-in, "just-in-time" help and support videos for teachers, students, and parents that may be accessed at any time (Figure 3).

Finally, feedback should always begin with a positive remark and be specific. It should also be supported by examples or evidence from the students' work. It is important that feedback should not include a grade, which is performance based. A mere number or letter grade does not help students understand why they did or did not do well and what they should improve on. It is equally important to encourage and support parents in providing comments on their children's work. Parents may not understand how to provide helpful and positive feedback. Students simply feel encouraged and supported knowing their parents have looked at their work; this is always a good start. In the ePEARL resources page, there is a guide for parents that directs them in how they can participate in the portfolio process and offers some guiding questions in providing feedback. All schools and teachers can prepare such resources.

After careful portfolio analysis, we have identified some examples of constructive and nonconstructive teacher, parent, and student feedback.

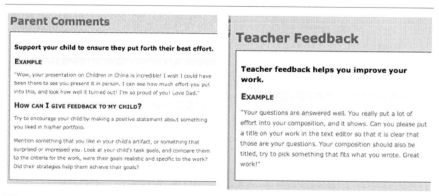

Figure 3. Help — Parent comments and teacher feedback

As seen in the examples in Table 1, students and parents need guidance in providing comments. Several students will make spelling mistakes and regard this feature as a "chat." It is up to the teacher to exemplify the type of feedback they want to see and discuss what they expect from students ahead of time.

LESSONS LEARNED

While teachers and their students see great promise in the use of EPs for learning, much remains to be done to ensure this promise is realized. To teach the skills of self-regulation within an EP environment requires commitment, purpose, and strategies on the part of teachers and students. It requires both "will" and "skill." Although EPs are designed to promote student learning and facilitate classroom communication, the software can't do this work alone. Teachers need to continually provide modeling and instruction to promote effective goal setting, feedback, and reflecting within the portfolio through structured lessons, discussions, and other classroom activities. Support materials for ePEARL, such as job aids, lesson plans, and instructional videos, are available to help educators effectively teach these skills.

Although the examples provided in this article speak most specifically to classroom practices tailored for teachers working with students in elementary and secondary classrooms, the principles of EP and its use in promoting effective classroom communications can also be applied in a postsecondary setting. Instructors working with students in the college or university setting can use software such as Moodle, blogs, easy web-page design sites such as Google Sites, and WebCT to facilitate the processes of setting goals, identifying strategies, creating work, revising, providing feedback, and reflecting on one's work. Although these tools don't provide the same type of structured guidance as ePEARL does, the instructor can model and provide prompts to students to stimulate the processes of setting goals, sharing work, providing constructive feedback, and reflecting on the learning process.

EPs can be particularly useful in larger classes where peer-to-peer interactions may be minimal or are limited to a vocal minority of students in the course. In such cases, it may be beneficial to assign students to smaller online discussion groups so they can interact with each other outside of class and keep the dialogue and learning space active on their own time. They can exchange ideas, as well as post assignments to give and receive feedback. This can help to build a greater sense of community among the

CONSTRUCTIVE FEEDBACK	NONCONSTRUCTIVE FEEDBACK
What tools can help you reach your goal? Did you re-read your work to check for punctuation? (Teacher)	Reading is an important goal! (Teacher) Keep up the awesome work! (Teacher)
I encourage you to remember your reflection when you start your next project. Making good choices is a smart strategy to try. (Teacher)	Blaise, congratulations on completing your first design challenge. Your grade is 55/55. (Teacher)
I think it is great that you are writing letters as your format for your zine article. I think you should continue to work on this entry and add some more details. Why did the school board decide to cancel summer vacation? (Teacher)	Sabrina, you did well on the second run. You have a few minor spelling errors to correct. Your grade is 53/55. (Teacher) Great reflection. I hope you enjoyed working on this project! (Teacher)
Punctuation is important when trying to convey your thoughts to your reader, Susan. You have noted where you need to improve and that is encouraging. You have self-assessed your writing weakness correctly and can now work on improving your writing style. (Parent)	Why is this not being used more? There is nothing in here and the year is almost over. (Parent)
Have thought of getting more info and not talking about Rune escape all the time but it had good pictures. (Student)	Nice job on the notes I like it so much it was cool. (Student)

Table 1. Sample feedback

students and to make the online communication more manageable and personal for the students. Creating some sort of interactive EP that supports self-regulated learning and aligns with the needs of your course and students is one way to stimulate classroom communication when the structure of the classes make interactive, face-to-face discussions difficult.

Web-based EPs provide a valuable platform for extending classroom "spaces" and learning dialogues. By catering to individual student's learning styles and paces, EPs can facilitate engagement with and contributions from all students, particularly those who might not feel confident participating verbally in class discussions or other fast-paced, face-to-face activities. It is important that educators tap into new technologies and new pedagogies to meet the changing needs of their students and classrooms. EPs can provide a new path to support the development of essential skills and foster new forms of communication for learning inside and beyond the classroom environment.

NOTE

1. LEARN stands for the Leading English Education and Resource Network. See http://www.learnquebec.ca/en/

REFERENCES

Abrami, Phillip C., and Helen Barrett. 2005. Directions for research and development on electronic portfolios. *Canadian Journal of Learning and Technology, 31*(3): 1–15.

Arter, Judith A., and Vicki Spandel. 1992. Using portfolios of student work in instruction and assessment. *Educational Measurement: Issues and Practice, 11*(1): 36–44.

MacIsaac, Doug, and Lewis Jackson. 1994. Assessment processes and outcomes: Portfolio construction. *New Directions for Adult and Continuing Education,* 62(Summer): 63–72.

Wade, Anne, Phillip C. Abrami, and Jennifer Sclater. 2005. An electronic portfolio to support learning. *Canadian Journal of Learning and Technology, 31*(3): 33–50.

Zimmerman, Barry, J. 1989. A social cognitive view of self-regulated academic learning. *Journal of Educational Psychology, 81*(3): 329–339.

Zimmerman, Barry, J. 2000. Attaining self-regulation: A social cognitive perspective. In Monique Boekaerts, Paul R. Pintrich, and Moshe Zeidner (Edes.), *Handbook of self-regulation,* (pp. 13–39). New York: Academic Press.

Zimmerman, Barry J., and Kallen E. Tsikalas. 2005. Can computer-based learning environments (CBLEs) be used as self-regulatory tools to enhance learning? *Educational Psychologist, 40*(4): 267–271.

Broadcollecting

Using personal response systems ("clickers") to transform classroom interaction

Tom Haffie

University of Western Ontario

There was a time when students were seen as empty buckets waiting to be filled with knowledge sprayed from a fire hose by a professor at the front of the lecture hall. Sometimes the lecture was even broadcast over closed-circuit networks, television, or the Web to ever larger, but inherently passive, audiences.

Personal response systems have changed all of that. These electronic devices transmit signals from individual students to instructors. Usually students are transmitting their answers to structured, multiple-choice or numerical questions posed during class. Receiver software on a classroom computer collects responses and then displays the data as a graph. Although all responses are anonymous in the room, systems can be configured to link responses to individual students. Records can be collected for subsequent analysis by instructors and/or students. Although previous generations of this technology have been in limited use for decades, recent development of handheld radio frequency units has resulted in widespread adoption in higher education. This technology, commonly referred to as "clickers," is consistently well received by students and instructors for the reasons I outline in this article (Barnett 2006; DeBourgh 2008; MacArthur and Jones 2008; Reay et al. 2005).

BROADCOLLECTING

Personal response systems enable a novel, potentially transformative type of interaction in the classroom, whether they are hardwired or based on infrared, radio frequency, cell phone, or wireless PDA/laptop transmitters.

This point is worth stressing—clickers invite teachers and learners into a type of encounter that neither experiences in any other aspect of their respective lives. When have you heard of, much less experienced, the collective voice of an audience addressing a single presenter *in real time*? This is the opposite of one-to-many broadcasting. But what is it called? We are all familiar with opinion polls, marketing surveys, and election voting, but these types of many-to-one systems are one-off events that seldom occur in real time. They are in no way "conversational." The "many" do not feel like they are partners in a discussion with the "one." I propose the new term "broadcollecting" to describe the process of listening and responding to the collective voice of an audience in real time. The ability to broadcollect using clickers now invites a creative counterpoint in the classroom whereby one instructor engages many students in a generative back-and-forth, question-and-answer, give-and-receive relationship that promises dramatic benefits for all concerned.

Instructors are habitually engaged in crafting environments that invite the elusive "teachable moment" in which the minds of students are open to change. I picture the minds of my students as supersaturated solutions swirling with previously learned ideas, thoughts, and attitudes. I see myself introducing a provocative new idea, a seed, around which new understanding can crystallize out of the chaos of previously unconnected or even misconceived ideas. As I describe below, the "conversation" established between the instructor and the class through alternating broadcasting/broadcollecting can conjure teachable moments by directing student attention, providing feedback on their understanding, guiding their thinking, confronting their misconceptions, instigating discussion, and monitoring the overall distribution of knowledge in the class. The perspective of this article begins with a narrow focus on the details of questioning and then expands to consider the rhythm of broadcollecting in a given lecture before closing with thoughts about curriculum design and supportive policy.

QUESTION DESIGN AND DELIVERY

It is important for students and instructors to understand that clickers are most powerful in the service of formative, rather than summative, assessment. Summative questions are designed primarily to discover what knowledge, skills, or attitudes a student possesses at a specific moment in a formal testing environment. However, formative questions are primarily designed to stimulate thinking that can be used for critique in a supportive learning environment. While the precision, clarity, and completeness of summative questions with unique answers tend to minimize the need for additional discussion, clicker questions are often deliberately vague, incomplete, or satisfied by more than one answer in order to stimulate thinking and provoke discussion. Therefore, good test questions rarely yield good clicker questions.

The classroom broadcollecting strategies described in the following list employ different types of questions at different times in a lecture to accomplish different goals. A question to begin a class may be a straightforward attempt to discover what students recall from a previous lecture or reading. However, a question designed to stimulate the discussion of a fundamental concept may need to be more thoughtfully structured. Beatty and colleagues (2006) point out that designing such questions is a challenge not to be taken lightly. They describe effective discussion questions as those that serve a content goal, a process goal, and a metacognitive goal. That is, questions are designed and posed with the multiple objectives: (a) to focus attention on fundamental content knowledge; (b) to encourage students to develop cognitive skills to use that knowledge to analyze, make predictions, and evaluate alternatives; and (c) to help students become aware of how practitioners of the discipline learn, think, and practice. They provide several sample questions, as well as "tactics" for question development and renovation. Overall, it is important to consider the objective(s) of each clicker question and to design it accordingly.

The pacing of the delivery dramatically influences the success of clicker questions in class. In general, I take control of the pacing to counteract the tendency of students to feel rushed by the clock and unable to think clearly. I have found it helpful to have a particular slide transition that introduces all clicker questions; students quickly begin reaching for their clickers automatically when this transition appears. Before allowing students to respond to a question, I explain the situation and clarify the alternative answers. Even after the voting has begun, I pause the process if anyone asks for clarification. I let the clock run down as the majority of answers come in.

Revealing the correct answer is an important step in the choreography of broadcollecting, and I plan this in advance for each question. In some situations, I allow the correct answer to be identified immediately as the answer distribution is displayed to the class. The discussion that follows could draw attention to the distribution itself. "Why would a class like this respond in this way?" However, since most of the questions are designed to support some sort of higher-level thinking and/or follow-up discussion, I initially withhold the correct answer in order to more fully consider all of the possible options.

It is important to bring closure to each question, and strategies for this should be considered in advance. If it is appropriate to "wrap-up" a given question, one could move through each successive answer, summarizing the ideas raised and demonstrating how experts reason through to the "correct" answer. Alternatively, students could be invited to defend alternative answers in a classwide discussion. Sometimes questions are best left unresolved to provide an out-of-class, follow-up challenge. In such cases, students could be referred to alternative sources and invited to either post solutions to an electronic course discussion board or come to the next class prepared to meet a similar question.

In the past, it was tempting for instructors to assume that, while they were teaching, students were learning. However, one of the potentially terrifying situations that can arise with broadcollecting is that instructors may discover that their inspired teaching of a concept had little effect on the learning in the class. This is a vulnerable position that I encourage colleagues to risk—but not without an "exit plan." Decide in advance what you will do if you find yourself faced with a class that clearly doesn't understand an important point in the lecture. You might go over the point again from a different perspective, come back to it at a later time, assign some reading or homework, or perhaps redirect the discussion to tutorial or online discussion.

BROADCOLLECTING STRATEGIES

In addition to the basic principles of sound question design and delivery, it is important to also consider the overall rhythm of the broadcasting/broadcollecting dialogue in a given lecture. The following strategies for broadcollecting range from standard didactic lectures enhanced by strategic questioning to radically new lecture styles that are "driven" by successive questioning cycles.

1. **Bookends:** Clicker questions can be used as a classroom management ritual to signal the beginning or end of class. Questions can focus attention on material to come, review outside reading, or link to other lectures.

2. **Punctuation:** Traditional lectures often have an iterative rhythm in which main concepts are introduced, expanded on,

and then linked to the next concept, which is then expanded on, and so on for the duration of class. Thoughtfully timed clicker questions can accentuate this rhythm, particularly by providing alternative stimulation as attention wavers.

3. **Shoot First …:** "Are there any questions?" Instructors who are trying to discover if their teaching has resulted in learning often use this tired questioning cliché. This strategy can, at best, generate insight into the understanding of only a few students—who are unlikely to be representative of the class as a whole. Well-crafted clicker questions are a much more effective tool for discovering how close students are to reaching learning outcomes at any given time in class.

4. **"A Class Full of Guinea Pigs":** Classroom demonstrations can be a refreshing opportunity to "show" a concept rather than "tell" it. Broadcollecting enables the instructor to engage students as subjects in real-time demonstrations. For instance, the data generated by a roomful of students flipping coins or reporting their height can illustrate various statistical principles (Duncan 2005, 35). Some clicker software allows the data from one question to be cross-tabulated with those of another question. This feature could be used to reveal sociodemographic trends such as gender-specific economic behavior or correlations between religious affiliation and scientific beliefs among members of the class.

I draw a line here. Although the previous four strategies for clicker use can be beneficial in the ways described, instructors who employ only these methods are likely to conclude that clickers are neither worth the expense nor the administrative overhead. I agree. The dramatic benefits of broadcollecting only accrue when clickers are used to frequently and consistently support critical thinking, peer interaction, and metacognitive growth among students through robust engagement with course material and one another. The following strategies illustrate how addressing more engaging pedagogies can transform the classroom.

5. **Question Sequences:** Instructional objectives often encourage students to move beyond "understanding" with content aimed at higher-order thinking involved in applying concepts, connecting new ideas to those already learned, and/or transferring understanding to novel situations. A sequence of clicker

questions, each directly following the other and each representing an increasing level of thinking, can create a "thinking ramp" that elevates the level of discussion in the classroom. The questions might first test vocabulary, then application of a concept, and then transfer of an idea to a novel situation.

Students may find the thinking ramp difficult if their initial learning is very context specific. To help reduce this constraint, another type of question sequence could be useful. If a series of (quick) questions is asked relating exactly the same concept to different conditions or variables, students will discover how a given concept can be generalized (Reay, Li, and Bao 2008).

6. **Classwide Discussion:** In this technique, a brief period of lecturing sets up a question. Students are invited to discuss the question in small groups of peers without any intent to come to consensus. Everyone then votes individually. In response to the distribution of answers, the instructor draws the class into a discussion. Why would this class have this distribution of answers? Would someone who answered "A" please share his or her reasoning? Once the important ideas have been discussed, the instructor can reveal the correct answer, bring closure to the discussion, and proceed to set up the next question or discussion (Nicol and Boyle 2003).

7. **Peer Instruction:** In the previous method, students discuss their reasoning with one another before they vote. The peer instruction method inverts this sequence. After the instructor presents a particular topic, he or she poses a question (perhaps designed to highlight a common misconception). Students initially develop an answer from their own mind and then vote without consulting peers. The displayed answer distribution then provides a context for peer discussion, during which participants attempt to convince one another of the soundness of their initial reasoning. Then, a second round of voting often reveals that the class distribution has shifted in favor of the correct answer. Instructors bring closure by modeling appropriate thinking to the correct answer. (This technique is usually most effective if the initial frequency of correct answers is between thirty and seventy percent). Lectures may be constructed as a series of minilessons followed by peer instruction (Crouch and Mazur 2001).

8. **Question-driven Instruction:** In the words of the developers of this technique, question-driven instruction "does more than augment traditional instruction: it forms the very core of the instructional dynamic" (Beatty et al. 2006, p. 32). In such a learning environment, students' first exposure to new material occurs in advance, outside the classroom. "Lectures" are presented as a cyclical series of question posing: peer discussion, voting, class discussion, and effective closure. Questioning is not preceded by teaching per se. In fact, traditional didactic lecturing occurs only on an as-needed basis to facilitate productive discussion. The success of this pedagogy develops the ability of the questions to evoke productive thinking in combination with the agility of the instructor in making this thinking available through discussion (Beatty et al. 2006).

9. **Clicker Cases:** Case studies are widely used tools to provide real-world context for course material and to encourage interactive learning and the development of higher-order thinking skills. Although it can be challenging to expand case-based teaching to large classes in fixed-seating auditoria, clickers can be a powerfully enabling technology in these situations (Herreid 2006). In particular, those cases that can be "interrupted" at key stages lend themselves to the use of clickers. Brickman (2006) describes an example involving DNA fingerprinting and forensics. Students can be asked how to interpret evidence, how they would proceed with the case, or what is the final conclusion. To borrow from methods previously described, questions could involve peerwide or classwide discussion before or after voting, and they could be sequenced as a thinking ramp.

PEDAGOGICAL BENEFITS

Regardless of the overall strategy used, broadcollecting with clickers can leverage the effectiveness of established teaching techniques and can introduce new strategies of engagement that result in benefits that include (Beatty 2004; Crouch and Mazur 2001; DeBourgh 2008; Reay, Li, and Bao 2008):

1. **Inclusivity:** My experience is that well over eighty percent of students participate in any given question. Students who may

be too shy or uncertain to speak in class can still enjoy the benefits of participation with their clicker. Engaging the majority of students in the class reduces classroom civility issues and sets the stage for productive peer interaction.

2. **Accountability:** The act of selecting and clicking a button is a commitment that, even if anonymous or unrecorded, creates accountability for one's actions. Students cannot easily dismiss the experience of their thinking leading them to an incorrect answer.

3. **Formative Assessment:** Feedback on clicker questions is typically immediate and in context. Students have the opportunity to see mistakes and, ideally, witness the instructor guiding the class through a thinking process that evaluates the alternatives while identifying the best answers. Also, feedback to instructors provides a commentary on the effectiveness of instructional strategies.

4. **Discussion:** Clickers facilitate pedagogies of engagement by making the collective students' thinking visible through the display of answer distributions. This display may then provoke discussion in any of several formats (e.g., think-pair-share, peer instruction, or classwide discussion). The function of a follow-up discussion is to further expose, evaluate, clarify, and extend the thinking on a particular topic. Students may be forced to reconcile their own understandings or explanations of the situation at hand with those of their peers.

5. **Metacognitive Development:** The simple presence of clickers in a classroom provides an opening for a conversation that draws attention to how learning occurs in lecture and how it can be promoted through specific strategies. Well-designed questions can encourage students to consider how they learn on a personal level as well as how they think through problems as novice practitioners of a particular discipline.

6. **Conceptual Understanding:** Several studies of pre- and post-testing with standardized instruments have revealed significantly improved gains in understanding among students who experience the type of classroom engagement supported by clickers (Crouch and Mazur 2001; Hake 1998; Reay, Li, and Bao 2008; also see the references cited within these sources.)

7. **Cumulative Record:** In cases where clicker responses are recorded and reported back to students on a regular basis, this growing body of formative assessment can motivate students to reconsider study habits and preparation for class (Haffie, Meadows, and Dawson 2007). Such critical evaluation of academic skills may be particularly relevant in the beginning weeks of the term, before the first round of summative testing.

8. **Coactive Lecturing:** Instructors can use information gleaned from broadcollecting to adapt lecture presentations "on the fly." Such adjustments may lead to lectures that more effectively complement the knowledge and ability of a particular class in a particular moment.

9. **Modeling Mastery Goals:** Many students in many classes are motivated by performance goals; they want to know the correct answers in order to get a good grade. However, in bringing closure to each episode of broadcollecting, instructors have the opportunity to model mastery goals. We have a captive audience for whom we can demonstrate how experts in our discipline think through problems. We can show that knowing why an answer is correct supports further learning much more than just knowing that it is correct.

DESIGN AND ADMINISTRATIVE CONSIDERATIONS

Broadcollecting, when used to its fullest potential, is a powerful catalyst for active engagement in the classroom. To be most effective, this strategy should be woven intimately into the curriculum design of a given course and enjoy supportive administrative policy. This article has shown that we do not adopt clickers just so we can tack a couple of questions onto the same lecture we have always given. We adopt clickers so that we can fundamentally change how our lectures are designed and presented in order to dramatically influence the quality of learning outcomes experienced by those who participate in it.

Supportive administrative policy can greatly improve how instructors and students experience the use of clickers. If this technology is unfamiliar to students, some introductory technical information should be provided along with an explanation of how the clickers will be used in the educational outcomes of the class. This is also a useful juncture to describe formative assessment and to coach students on how to best make use of the feedback provided by clickers in class. Course information should clearly state if, or how, clicker responses will contribute to final grades. If clicker responses are recorded and contribute a "participation" grade, it is wise for instructors to build in some "flexibility." That is, students might be required to participate in only 80 percent of the questions in order to earn 100 percent of the participation grade. This flexibility provides automatic accommodation for a wide range of issues (medical or compassionate absences, technical glitches, forgotten hardware, etc.) that can otherwise accumulate into a substantial administrative overhead. In my experience, requiring students to choose the correct answer in order to earn participation credit undermines much of the value of clickers. Students feel like they now have a test in every class and are less likely to engage in the type of risky divergent thinking that is pedagogically productive. Regardless of the end use, clicker responses should be afforded the same degree of security, confidentiality, and transparency that is customary for test grades.

Since clickers are only distinguishable by internal serial numbers, and because they can often be operated in a concealed manner, opportunities for academic impersonation will arise. Course information should be clear that use of more than one clicker, or of a clicker that is not one's own, constitutes an academic offense.

CONCLUSION

Personal response systems enable "broadcollecting"—a novel type of many-to-one communication—that, in combination with traditional one-to-many broadcasting, can result in a type of conversation between instructors and the class as a whole that transforms the conventional lecture. See the "For Further Reflection and Action" section at the end of the book for guidance to help you include clickers into class discussion. Broadcollecting is a widely participatory, highly active and engaging pedagogic strategy that can result in significant learning gains.

REFERENCES

Barnett, John. 2006. Implementation of personal response units in very large lecture classes: student perceptions. *Australasian Journal of Educational Technology*, 22(4): 474–94.

Beatty, Ian D. 2004. Transforming student learning with classroom communication systems. Educause Center for Applied Research. *Research Bulletin ERB0403* (3): 1–15.

Beatty, Ian D., William J. Gerace, William J. Leonard, and Robert J. Dufresne. 2006. Designing effective questions for classroom response system teaching. *American Journal of Physics*, 74(1): 31–39.

Brickman, Peggy. 2006. The case of the Druid Dracula: A directed "clicker" case study on DNA fingerprinting. *Journal of College Science Teaching*, 36(October): 48–53.

Crouch, Catherine, and Eric Mazur. 2001. Peer instruction: Ten years of classroom experience and results. *American Journal of Physics*, 69(9): 970–977.

DeBourgh, Gregory A. 2008. Use of classroom "clickers" to promote acquisition of advanced reasoning skills. *Nurse Education in Practice*, 8(2): 76–87.

Duncan, Douglas. 2005. *Clickers in the classroom: How to enhance science teaching using classroom response systems.* San Francisco: Pearson Education.

Haffie, Tom L., Ken N. Meadows, and Debra Dawson. 2007. Engaging students in their own learning: The influence of cumulative clicker performance on students' learning strategy use and academic achievement. Poster presented at the annual conference of the Society for Teaching and Learning in Higher Education (STLHE), June 13–17 in Edmonton, Canada.

Hake, Richard R. 1998. Interactive-engagement versus traditional methods: A six-thousand-student survey of mechanics test data for introductory physics courses. *American Journal of Physics*, 66(1): 64–74.

Herreid, Clyde Freeman. 2006. "Clicker" cases: Introducing case study teaching into large classrooms. *Journal of College Science Teaching*, 36(October): 43–47.

MacArthur, James R., and Loretta L. Jones. 2008. A review of literature reports of clickers applicable to college chemistry classrooms. *Chemistry Education Research and Practice*, 9(3): 187–195.

Nicol, David J., and James T. Boyle. 2003. Peer Instruction versus class-wide discussion in large classes: A comparison of two interaction methods in the wired classroom. *Studies in Higher Education*, 28(4): 457–473.

Reay, Neville W., Lei Bao, Pengfei Li, Rasil Warnakulasooriya, and Gordon Baugh. 2005. Toward the effective use of voting machines in physics lectures. *American Journal of Physics*, 73(6): 554–558.

Reay, Neville W., Pengfei Li, and Lei Bao. 2008. Testing a new voting machine question methodology. *American Journal of Physics*, 76(2): 171–178.

Podcast

A tool to pique curiosity, evoke a response, and create opportunities for student engagement

Dave Yearwood
University of North Dakota

Advances in audio/visual technologies have resulted in miniature electronic devices (e.g., mp3/mp4 players) capable of allowing anyone to be simultaneously connected with others, engaged, entertained, and also distracted. These portable electronic marvels make it possible for individuals and businesses to deliver podcasts in different formats: audio only, a blend of audio with static and dynamic images, with video, computers, cell phones, MP3 players, and personal digital assistants. Given that the university campus is a microcosm of the general population at large, there is the likelihood that visitors to institutions of higher education will encounter students, faculty, staff, and possibly administrators who are plugged in, connected to, or at the very least preoccupied with some technology. If the preoccupation observed is a basic human trait or desire, then to what extent can an individual's predisposition to engagement be manipulated in the classroom to promote meaningful interactions at multiple levels: between faculty and students, students and their peers, and all with the content? Further, how can podcasts—essentially a redesigned tool of a bygone era begun with wax or vinyl records and spooled tape—be reformulated for educational purposes? Educators are hardly newcomers to technology, but a clear understanding of podcasts is essential if faculty want to connect with, engage, and enhance student learning through their use of podcasts.

PODCASTING:
HISTORY AND IDENTIFYING ELEMENTS

Podcasting is a relatively new term that owes it origin to Web-logs, commonly known as blogs—a way for individuals to share text-based content via the Internet on just about any topic to any audience. Blogs, which prior to 2001 (the period when Apple launched its iPod and the transition to recorded audio began to gain more prominence) (Burrows 2007) were largely typed text, soon gave way to an enhanced version called audio blogs. This technology was aided by several individuals, such as: Ben Hammersely, whom many credit as the person who coined the term "podcasting" when he made mention of it in a Guardian article published February 12, 2004 (Hammersley 2004); Adam Cury, an MTV personality and blogger (Campbell 2005); and Dave Winer (Lauria 2006), a software developer who developed a method whereby content posted on the Web could be automatically identified and downloaded. However, the term, "podcast" really gained notoriety when the New Oxford American Dictionary (Oxford University Press 2005) named "podcast" as its word of the year. Further, the proliferation of MP3 players popularized by Apple's iPod and developments in technology related to RSS feeds, compression schemes, faster computer processors, portable or net computers, and wideband access soon made it possible and easier for the general public to retrieve audio content that they could listen to anytime, anyplace.

A Google search of the word "podcast" on the Internet returned 132,000,000 hits when this article was written, and the expectation is that this number will continue to increase significantly due to the ease with which one can create, publish, and retrieve podcasts. But, at its very core, the podcast is hardly a recent phenomenon since the radio—both live and recorded—made it possible for listeners to enjoy audio *when* it was being broadcast. However, the *when* imposed a time constraint for individuals who, if they wanted to listen to a particular audio broadcast must, by necessity, commit to a specific location, tune in, and then listen to some specific content when it was being beamed over the airways—a synchronous activity—or alternatively, to make arrangements to record the transmitted message. However, the Internet changed all of this by allowing recorded content to be stored on servers where they could be retrieved for use at the listener's convenience—an asynchronous activity. Additionally, the development of portable digital audio/video players and other technological advances relating to Really Simple Syndication (RSS) feeds further frees the listener in terms of time and place, thus ushering in the concept of "on-demand" Web-based programming.

Podcasts are typically fashioned around the established practices of broadcast style programming for radio and television. They are packaged for the Internet and delivered to computers and portable media devices. Today, many individuals, businesses, news organizations—particularly National Public Radio (NPR)—hospitals, and the education field offer a variety of podcasts to targeted audiences free of cost. As with everything in the technology arena, podcasters were not satisfied with audio-only content and soon devised a method for delivering two additional types, enhanced and video podcast or vodcast. Of the three types of podcasts, the most popular is the audio variety—MP3 format—but video content in MP4 format has gained some popularity, and the latest incarnation of portable media (including mini notebook computers) now makes it possible for users to listen or view video podcasts—podcast with static images called "enhanced" podcasts and video podcasts consisting of dynamic images combined with audio.

Receiving podcasts requires that the user either: (a) surfs the Web to locate a specific podcast of interest they can then download to their computer, or (b) start a subscription to an RSS feed—a protocol that automates the process of downloading specific podcasts to their computer. The RSS feed is the preferred method for receiving podcasts because it automates the entire process of obtaining and downloading content in a similar manner to a magazine or newspaper subscription, where the reader can simply receive future publications on a regular basis at certain intervals without ever leaving their homes. For nonsubscribers, however, the only method by which the user can receive current publications is for them to physically locate and retrieve the magazine or newspaper from a kiosk or other location. The key difference between the two is the convenience factor in which one system, the subscription service, is automated and the product is delivered to your computer every time you start the pod-catching or aggregator program. Someone who does not subscribe to RSS feeds can only receive podcasts by surfing the Web to locate each podcast and then download it to their computer. Two of the most popular aggregators are iTunes and Juice, for both Windows and Apple, but other podcast aggregators include Doppler, Podcast Alley, and Podcast Pickle.

To start a subscription, users simply download and install one of many free aggregator software programs into their computer. Next, they will navigate directly to the podcast or download section of their respective aggregator and select the podcasts they wish to subscribe to. The method for starting a podcast subscription is rather simple, and anyone familiar with using computers programs should have no difficulty because of the intuitive nature of the process. A software program is usually required to play any downloaded podcast, and there are many free programs available such as Quicktime, iTunes, or Windows Media Player. For PC users, the obvious choice may be Windows Media Player to both listen to and sync podcasts to portable media players. The power and simplicity of iTunes is that it seamlessly functions as both the aggregator and the player, thus making it the program of choice for many who listen to podcasts. Further, downloaded podcasts can be synched to any iPod using the Mac or Windows version of iTunes.

BASIC APPEAL AND REQUIRED KNOWLEDGE

The basic attraction of podcasting may center around three entities that appeal to twenty-first-century students: most podcasts are free; they are portable; and they create feelings of connectedness. The feeling of connectedness comes from the fact that the podcaster is, in effect, sharing information in a somewhat private setting, thus creating a one-on-one bond with the listener. Another related appeal of podcasts may lie in what Campbell (2005, 40) calls the "magic in human voice [to persuade/convince, and entice students], the magic of shared awareness." Therefore, it stands to reason that if language (visual, such as sign language and symbols, and auditory) is one of several keys to the human mind, then it seems logical to assume that any of the three types of podcasts (audio, enhanced, and video) might be excellent media for connecting with students and engaging them in some activity of mutual interest. However, not all podcasts are created equal. Just as the quality of videos posted to YouTube and/or TeacherTube vary significantly, podcasts are also subject to variation of quality. Podcasts developed with little consideration to precisely what is to be communicated, how information should be presented, or the need to convey a sense of passion about the content could do more harm than good.

Podcasts, when properly developed, provide opportunities for faculty and students to explore course content beyond what might be possible in traditional classroom settings. The operative word here is *properly*, since the application of any tool places an onus on the producer to ensure that the podcast achieves the desired effect independent of its applicability—improve safety, increase efficiency and productivity, reduce costs, and from an educational perspective, enhance or improve student understanding. All too often, educators lose sight of the primary goal, and the resulting effect is that the tool draws more attention to itself rather than helping focus attention on the content. Similarly, a focus on the tool itself may place some restraints on the instructor's ability to use the technology to create an atmosphere of engagement with those in shared learning spaces. The extent to which a tool can be used to meet a desired academic objective requires more than a mere understanding of hardware and software by the user; further, many users fail to note this important distinction in their fascination with technologies of one variety or another.

Tools utilized for the business sector cannot simply be adopted by faculty and put to use in the classroom. A healthy dose of creativity and pedagogical understanding is essential if students are to acquire, process, and use information in meaningful ways. Educators must be purposeful and selective in their use of podcasts or any collection of technological tools. In essence, focusing on how students learn is perhaps the one thing that should most influence our teaching (National Research Council 2002). Therefore, faculty wishing to use podcasts as an instructional tool must address several important issues: the composition of the audience, the purpose of the instruction, the purpose of their podcast, the added value contribution of the podcast, and how to maintain students' interest in their podcasts—if they hope to achieve the desired goal of increased learning. None of these steps will be easy to implement, but to exclude any in a discussion about teaching and learning, particularly how selected tools will benefit students, is to place the carriage before the horse. Faculty need to recognize that they are the *education technology gatekeepers*, a responsibility that they should not abdicate to Information Technology (IT) personnel, the business community, or technological zealots. Further, any discussion about podcasts *must* also consider the extent to which this specific tool will enhance student learning by adding something to the teaching and learning environment that would otherwise not be possible; the ease with which one could integrate selected tools into their practice; and the extent to which there is a fit of one's teaching style to a given technology.

The matter of fit is extremely important when considering the applicability of selected tools. An audio podcast may not be the best fit for a mathematics teacher who utilizes the chalkboard or whiteboard to illustrate concepts or demonstrate how to dissect a problem in an effort to arrive at a solution. Clearly, the preferred option would be either enhanced podcasts or vodcasts. Technological tools by themselves will not necessarily make one a better teacher in the same way that access to tools cannot make one a skilled worker. But the matter of fit applies not only to the teacher. If the primary reason for creating a podcast is to improve teaching *and* learning, then the focus *must* be on the student and how a particular technology can be used to promote cognition (Mayer 2001). Similarly, skeptics of technology need to confront their fears, apprehension, or phobia about technology use in academe while at the same time giving consideration to its potential. Personal biases and anecdotal evidence about technology utilization in teaching and learning is no substitute for refusing to acknowledge the potential of twenty-first-century tools, the same tools that are very much a part of our students' lives. Junco and Mastrodicasa (2007) suggest that digital native learners "prefer processing pictures, sound and video before text"; however, their digital immigrant teachers "prefer to provide text before pictures, sound and video." If this statement is true, then perhaps it would make sense for those in education to find a way to tap into students' preferences for pictures, sound, and video—all elements of enhanced podcasts and vodcasts—wherever and whenever such technologies would benefits learners.

Educators need to exploit the many possible avenues for using podcasts to engage students with the content, provide opportunities for expanded dialogue about what is contained in the podcast, and perhaps, even as a way to disseminate relevant but timely information. Reading, suggests Campbell (2005), is a difficult thing to do while walking [and driving], yet some individuals persists in this activity; but by contrast, listening to a podcast is very easy to do.

FACULTY CONCERNS

The introduction of any technology in education is always viewed with skepticism. This was the case with film when it was first introduced, with television, the Internet, PowerPoint, and now with podcasts and vodcasts. Some apprehension may be warranted, and indeed should be encouraged, as long as faculty can keep an open mind and are, at the very least, willing to consider discussions about the efficacy of technological tools. For example, the introduction and use of PowerPoint in academe was—and still is—met with much apprehension as educators feared that students would skip classes because the PowerPoint handouts contained just about everything that was covered in their presentations. Perhaps students who skipped class did so because they perceived that there was no added value to them being in class! This use of PowerPoint adds little to the teaching and learning environment, and under these conditions, the criticism about PowerPoint may indeed be warranted. Podcasts and vodcasts of entire lectures may lead to similar beliefs that if the lecture is made available to students, then why should they come to class? Young (2008) suggests several possible avenues available to faculty: have more interactivity in class; have more in-class quizzes; turn off the audio feed or camera at some point during the lecture and provide test-related information only to those in attendance; or, inform the entire class that if attendance drops below a certain percentage then no podcast or vodcast content will be posted. These are all valid suggestions designed to send a specific message to students—there is a penalty for missing class. But, should educators go to such extremes just to promote attendance? The tools of the podcast and vodcast should be a *supplement* to instruction rather than becoming objects of attraction and attention. The practice of developing instruction centered on the student reduces the possibility that any technology will draw attention to itself, shift the focus of attention away from the community of learners, and devalue the teaching process.

ESSENTIAL ELEMENTS OF GOOD PODCASTS

While just about anyone can produce a podcast, not everyone *should* create podcasts. Creating quality podcasts requires at a minimum, a modest investment of: time, equipment, careful planning and preparation, some technical expertise to record, edit, and post podcasts, and also an environment that is relatively noise free when recording. The previously listed items should be given careful consideration, as each directly impacts the quality of any created podcast. Those creating podcasts for educational purposes need to be held to a higher standard than someone who posts a personal blog to the Internet because one's professional reputation and that of the wider community of scholars may be at stake. Thus, a need exists for some degree of "podcast literacy," particularly as it pertains to pedagogical competency.

Therefore, any podcast created should have to pass a certain litmus test, beginning with the following:

- The purpose of—the reason for using—the podcast should be very clear to the listener.
- What are the objectives—the outcome—of the podcasts?
- Who will be served by the podcast should be readily apparent, and the same can be said about its value to the listener.

- What type of podcast to develop—audio only, enhanced, or video podcast—as this may require specialized equipment for both the producer and listener.
- The frequency of developed podcasts—how often can students expect to have a new podcast?
- Whether podcasts will feature several individuals—discussion format—or feature the instructor who might wish to have a conversational-type session, or whether the podcast will simply be a recording of the professor's lectures.

Each of the previous points are important issues to consider as they collectively keep the focus on teaching and learning where it belongs, rather than focusing on the technological bells and whistles. Educators need to ask themselves the all-important question regarding the use of podcasts: what is or will be the *value-added component* of using podcasting technologies? Simply recording one's lectures without first considering the value-added component might lead to wasted time on the faculty's part and possibly the learners as well.

Many educators mistakenly assume that students are knowledgeable about modern technologies, but this may not always be the case (Cockerline 2006). Nontraditional students—mostly older students—might not be as technologically savvy as their younger counterparts and, as a result, may not have similar technologies (i.e., portable media players, Personal Digital Assistants, other Wi-Fi devices, etc.). Further, why spend time developing enhanced podcasts or vodcasts if you are catering to students who have an extended commute to class? Perhaps an audio podcast might be more appealing because a distracted driver poses a serious problem to himself or herself and those in the immediate vicinity. One important finding worthy of mentioning pertains to the technology that podcast downloaders use to listen to podcasts; instructors should not assume that those who access their podcasts will listen to them on portable players (e.g., iPods, Zune, Creative Zen, etc.). In fact, in two separate studies by Cockerline and Nantais (2009) and Evans (2007) found that students on average, over seventy percent, listened to podcasts on their computers. This fact may not necessarily alter how the podcasts are created, however, it may influence whom podcasts are marketed to.

THE PODCASTS PRODUCTION CYCLE

Audio podcasting requires just a few simple pieces of equipment, but the choice of devices may vary between users and also the type of podcast being produced. A simple or basic setup requires a microphone for capturing audio content, some recording medium, and a computer with audio software for editing and mixing—removing parts of the recorded audio and/or inserting background music. Anyone considering enhanced podcasts or vodcasts will need to have some type of video editing software to stitch together the various graphical or video pieces which can then be stored on your computer, or more specifically, a server, and special computer programs can be used to generate an RSS feed for the now completed podcast. A more complete podcast system may utilize large condenser microphones (for better sound quality), an audio mixer for multiple microphones, and audio and/or video recording and editing software. Higher quality microphones will yield better quality audio, but these units cost substantially more. The following are some suggestions to get you started on your first podcast.

- Develop a plan that includes some specifics about the approximate length of the podcast, what the objectives will be, and how each objective will be addressed. The latter is intended to provide a sense of direction and guidance about the order in which the essentials of your podcast will be covered. The information collected should also be viewed from the perspective of helping you set the tone and tenor of your podcast.

- The general questions *who*, *what*, *when*, *where*, and *why*, as well as the *how* of your podcast are a proven journalistic approach that could be employed to help provide direction for your podcast. The information obtained should later be examined in light of the objectives and goals for your podcast.

- Concept mapping may be a useful tool to logically order the content to be addressed, who will be involved, the equipment to be used, and this information may also aid in the development of an introduction designed to capture the learner's attention while engaging them with the topic.

- A final part of the preproduction plan should include a list of questions to help guide the discussion or interview, as these are crucial to the success of the podcast. Deviation from the created script should not be an option, at least for the first few podcasts. Similarly, ad-libbing should be avoided unless this is something you are sure you have mastered. Even experienced podcasters follow some guide in an attempt to minimize their postproduction work.

Podcasting "gives professors a chance to meet students on their own turf," suggests Read (2007, 32). The reality is that since the twenty-first century, students appear as though they were born with various technologies attached to their bodies, so perhaps faculty could capitalize on their students' predisposition to technology by making course content readily available to them anytime, anyplace. But the reality is that recording podcasts requires some essential tools, and this creates a dilemma for faculty with limited podcast literacy skills. While recording podcasts might be a relatively simple activity, mastering the equipment at the same time that you are recording presents some interesting challenges for those unfamiliar with the technology, but this can be easily overcome with practice. The challenging part may be the posting of the completed podcast to a server where it can be accessed and downloaded by students. Because most colleges, universities, or K–12 schools have technical support, then perhaps the necessary training or assistance could be provided until a certain confidence level is reached. Campbell (2005) suggests teaming up with an instructional technology and audiovisual specialist rather than attempting to do it all. Alternatively, perhaps student assistance could be secured in the beginning stages until the instructor is knowledgeable enough to perform all of the required physical acts of recording and editing podcasts: set up the equipment to record, adjust sound levels, pay attention to lighting, frame video elements, and edit and post the podcast. Keep in mind that listeners or viewers to any podcast will judge the quality of the podcast on the basis of the audio and video quality, what is presented, how the content is sequenced, and what they perceive as the underlying purpose of the podcast to them. Therefore, anyone wishing to create podcasts should subscribe to one or more podcasts in an attempt to better understand how they are structured (i.e., determine who the target audience might be, the purpose of the podcast, how the podcast is organized or sequenced, persuasion factor of the podcast, quality of the recorded audio and video, etc.). The information gleaned from undertaking this activity is invaluable, and it could also help make your podcast more meaningful to listeners.

Someone commenting on technology and society on a TV show said that, "Technology will not make things better, it will just make things different!" There are many possibly ways to look at this statement and per- haps it may have to do with one's perspective. Medically speaking, technology may make life better by improving the quality of life for a para- plegic, for someone who requires dialysis treatment, or for someone who needs a pacemaker. But will technology make education better? Educa- tional tools matter, but not at the expense of student-centered instruc- tion! Educational tools should serve a specific purpose, they should help students see things in unique ways, and they could be used to challenge students. Podcasts could help educators achieve a number of educational goals, but are they a suitable substitute or replacement for instruction?

PODCAST EQUIPMENT AND OTHER GENERAL RECOMMENDATIONS

A variety of equipment and software is available to faculty, some at educa- tional discounts that make them very attractive. The equipment and soft- ware covered in the following paragraphs are not the only ones available, but I would suggest that you review what is mentioned carefully to see what might work for your particular situation. Additionally, this should not be considered an endorsement of any manufacture's product because no compensation was provided for including any of the products identified.

The minimum equipment needed for an audio podcast, for one indi- vidual, includes a microphone (preferably a condenser microphone, most of which are XLR-type microphones) and a computer with audio editing software. Keep in mind that External Line Return (XLR) microphones will require a mixer because this microphone connector cannot be directly plugged into a computer. However, there are Universal Serial Bus (USB) microphones available, and some of these work quite well. Alternatively, you could use a USB headset–microphone combination unit that connects directly to your computer. Audacity, a brand of free audio editing software, can be used to edit and mix voice and/or background music. If your goal is to create enhanced podcasts, then you might consider adding a program such as ProFCast (a Mac program with a Windows version due to be re- leased soon). ProFCast allows the user to complete a variety of tasks, and the software is thought of as an all-in-one program able to do the following: record a live presentation; synchronize PowerPoint slides with any audio; generate the RSS enclosure needed for automating the download of podcasts; and integrate easily with other Mac programs. Personally, ProF- Cast performed as advertised and the availability of a Windows version will be a welcome addition for PC users. Camtasia Studio is Windows software

157

that works well to create a podcast, but it currently lacks the ability to create RSS feeds. SnapKast is one of few Windows podcast software that is fairly simple to use and is somewhat comparable to ProFCast.

If your goal is to create audio podcast with a small group, then consider adding a microphone mixer like Korg's digital recording studio D888, which has a built-in 40-gigabyte hard drive, 8 microphone inputs, and a USB interface. There are other units available, like Zoom's portable MRS-8, but this unit only accepts two microphone inputs. Both the Krog and Zoom units work well, and the included hard drive in the Krog unit makes it convenient for recording audio (voice or instruments) without a computer; the Zoom unit uses a Secure Digital (SD) memory card for storage. Keep in mind that a directional microphone is the preferred choice for individual voice recordings, but omnidirectional microphones that can be shared with others in a group session might be a preferred option if cost is a consideration. Making a recording with several individuals will add an element of complexity (i.e., the need to edit the recorded audio to remove unnecessary noises). Audacity, the free audio editing software for multiple platforms mentioned in the previous paragraph, can be used to mix–edit, delete, or enhance-audio tracks if needed.

Another unit worthy of consideration is M-Audio's Podcast Factory, which includes an XLR microphone, a microphone stand, Audacity, and a USB connection for the computer. M-Audio's MicroTrack 24/96 device, a portable device that accepts 1/4-inch line or 1/8-inch microphone inputs, could also be used for recorded podcasts that are stored on a Compact-Flash (CF) memory card. One last thing to keep in mind: if a decision is made to go with dynamic microphones due to cost considerations, you should think about using a pop filter screen to eliminate "p" popping sounding words. A cheap alternative to a pop filter is a stocking, which works about as well as some pop filters.

If your podcast involves a small group of content experts who meet regularly to talk about various issues, you should take some time to carefully select individuals who can work well together and who complement each other. There should only be one coordinator or facilitator who is responsible for guiding the conversation or discussion. Likewise, encourage members to follow the developed script and resist the temptation to go off script or for anyone other than the facilitator to pose questions not related to what is being discussed. It is important that what the listener hears represents a group effort, rather than two or three different threads of disjointed content.

Finally, there is an issue that warrants some additional emphasis and further consideration, particularly by administration—department and college—and this pertains to levels of support and responsibility for faculty use of classroom tools. The production costs associated with podcast technology should not be borne by individual faculty, and similarly, technical support should be provided to individuals who see benefit in using classroom tools to aid instruction. Further, assistance should also be provided for faculty to obtain the necessary training that will allow them to use classroom tools in a pedagogically responsible manner. There are indeed appropriates ways to use instructional tools to capture students' attention, promote student engagement, and enhance teaching and learning. Faculty will indeed accomplish more when they are able to fully utilize classroom tools to achieve purposeful learning.

CONCLUSION

A certain degree of podcast literacy is essential if faculty hope to utilize audio- and video-based tools as academic supplements to connect with, engage, and encourage students to take a more active role in their education. The use of podcasts for educational purposes must have specific goals and objectives and must use proven pedagogical practices. Educational podcasts must have an identifiable, value-added component, one that results in increased student understanding about what is shared with them. Educational tools *can* make a difference in teaching and learning, but their utilization requires creativity, more than cursory knowledge about the tool and its potential, and any use of an educational tool requires a commitment on the part of faculty to create academic environments that focus on and promote student-centered learning.

REFERENCES

Burrows, Terry. 2007. *Blogs, wikis, MySpace, and more.* Chicago: Chicago Review Press.

Campbell, Gardner. 2005. There is something in the air: Podcasting in education. *Educause Review,* 40(6): 32–47.

Cockerline, Glenn. 2006. Cognitive styles in student use, perception, and satisfaction with online learning. Unpublished doctoral dissertation, University of North Dakota.

Cockerline, Glen, and Mike Nantais. 2009. Digital natives: How ICT-ready are our teacher candidates? (PowerPoint Slides). Paper presented at the Science, Mathematics, Technology, Teaching and Learning MERN/CRYSTAL research forum, February 6, in Winnipeg, Canada.

Evans, Chris. 2007. The effectiveness on m-learning in the form of podcast revision lectures in higher education. *ScienceDirect Computers & Education, 50*(2): 491–498.

Hammersley, Ben. 2004. Why online radio is booming. *The Guardian.* Available online at http://www.guardian.co.uk/media/2004/feb/12/broadcasting.digitalmedia.

Junco, Reynol, and Jeanna Mastrodicasa. 2007. *Connecting to the net generation: What higher education professionals need to know about today's student.* Washington, DC: NASPA.

Lauria, Vincent. 2006. *Introduction to syndication, (RSS) really simple syndication.* IBM. Available online at http://www-128.ibm.com/developerworks/xml/library/x-rssintro/.

Mayer, Richard. 2001. *Multimedia learning.* Cambridge, UK: Cambridge University Press.

National Research Council. 2002. *How people learn: Brain, mind, experience and school.* Washington, DC: National Academy Press.

Oxford University Press. 2005. *"Podcast" is the word of the year.* Accessed February 3, 2009, from http://www.oup.com/us/brochure/NOAD_podcast/?view=usa.

Read, Brock. 2007. How to podcast campus lectures. *The Chronicle of Higher Education, 53*(2): A32.

Young, Jeffrey. 2008. The lecturers are recorded so why go to class. *The Chronicle of Higher Education, 54*(36): A1.

Part Four

Assessing Students' Engagement

Assessment of Online Participation

Denise Stockley
Queen's University
Wendy Freeman
Ryerson University

Opportunities that encourage students to communicate with each other online can enhance a face-to-face class or extend one that is completely online. However, experience has shown that creating such an environment (e.g., a discussion forum or wiki) does not guarantee participation, as students are too often tasked with other courses, assignments, and extracurricular demands. Yet, we know students who engage with each other and the course material learn more deeply, and the question remains of how to encourage this type of behavior. Within this article we offer a variety of approaches that will provide avenues for students to participate online and various assessment techniques that can be used as a gateway for students to engage in the course and with each other.

PURPOSES OF ONLINE PARTICIPATION

Online course content that is static (i.e., no student interaction) often serves as a repository of information—neither encouraging nor permitting students to add or build knowledge. Students who visit these types of courses typically scan them at a surface level, often without making necessary connections outside of the online environment. This type of repository is useful for providing ideas and content but does not encourage students to deeply engage with the material. Just as important, students engaging with each other online are at the heart of a learning community, and this connection can also:

- Assist in the knowledge building process
- Promote deep learning

- Create a sense of responsibility and accountability toward their peers
- Encourage time management and planning skills
- Enhance interpersonal communication, including an awareness of others' viewpoints
- Allow for conflict negotiation and resolution

We have recognized the importance of online participation toward learning, now we need to now turn our attention to the different types of technology and their associated assessment techniques.

SYNCHRONOUS AND ASYNCHRONOUS ONLINE PARTICIPATION

Students participate online through an ever-changing array of technologies. Typically, the most common technology options are described as synchronous (when students and instructor are logged-in at the same time) or asynchronous (in which course participants contribute according to their own schedules). Each online technology supports a range of different types of participation, and therefore assessment methods are similarly diverse. In this section we review some of the technologies that are more frequently used to facilitate online participation, paying attention to the specific assessment issues that arise. This is not meant to be an exhaustive list, rather we hope to highlight the diversity of technologies that an instructor can incorporate in their course to encourage online participation.

SYNCHRONOUS TECHNOLOGIES

Online technologies that allow users to be logged in and communicating at the same time are referred to as *synchronous*. Synchronous technologies include chat, instant messaging (IM), web conferencing, and virtual environments, such as Second Life. In general, when assessing participation in synchronous environments, access is an important issue for consideration. Because students need to be logged-in at the same time, time zones, computer access, and in some cases the level of technology all play a role in the level of participation possible.

Chat and IM

Chat and IM are both technologies in which users communicate by typing text. Chat applications are widely available in most course management systems and can have multiple users logged in and chatting at one time. Chat is often used for brief discussions and for planning sessions. Students can use chat to plan assignments, discuss course topics, and even hold seminars. Some teachers use chat for lectures, small group discussions, or for office hours. Most chat tools have the option of saving a transcript of the session for later review.

Web Conferencing

There are a growing number of tools available for online audio and/or video conferencing. These tools can be used for real-time audio and video conferencing from the desktop. In addition, they frequently support application sharing and group presentations. Assessing participation in web conferences is similar to assessing participation in the face-to-face classroom.

With web conferencing, issues of access are of particular relevance because connections are not always reliable or stable, especially when video is being used. When participation is being assessed, students may experience stress related to the challenges posed by the technology that can interfere with learning. If you plan to use a web conferencing environment, alternatives for the technology or even the activity should be considered in case students have difficulty connecting.

Virtual Environments

Virtual environments can display the online space graphically, and participants can take on various physical appearances (avatars). Virtual environments, such as Second Life, provide students and teachers with the opportunity to interact, build communities, view and post course material, and even create and display shared objects online.

Virtual environments can be used to accommodate a wide range of learning outcomes; therefore, assessment of student participation can be tied to community building, collaboration, communication skills, and quality and quantity of participation, depending on the goals for the activity and the design of the activity itself.

ASYNCHRONOUS TECHNOLOGIES

Online technologies that support communication when course participants are logged in at different times are called *asynchronous*. Asynchronous technologies include online discussions forums, blogs, and wikis.

Online Discussions

Threaded discussion tools are commonly available and widely used in both distance and blended courses. There are many best practice guides and grading rubrics available for assessing participation in online discussion environments. With the proper structuring of discussion and timely and careful feedback, computer-mediated discussion has been found to support deep learning and community formation. Some distance courses rely almost exclusively on online discussion as the primary form of class participation. Therefore, assessment strategies that encourage participation are essential.

Course learning objectives can guide you in terms of what and how you can assess online participation. Participation in online discussion can take up a great deal of time. Reading others' contributions and preparing a response or an initial post all require frequent participation and thoughtful consideration to be effective. Therefore, an important consideration is to ensure that the weight of the grade assigned for the activity should be consistent with the effort required.

Blogs

A blog is a web-based tool that presents entries on a web site in reverse chronological order. Blogs can be an individual or group activity and have been used in courses as online journals, as group writing environments (e.g., a class newsletter), to document field experiences, or by teachers to post course information. Text, images, links, audio and video clips, and a growing range of other types of content can be easily posted on a blog. As with the assessment of other forms of online participation, the focus of assessment within a blogging environment is dependent on the goals you have for assigning the blogs as a learning activity. Because blogging can be an unfamiliar task for some students, they might need to be encouraged through assessment strategies that require active levels of participation. Additionally, unlike online discussion environments, blogs are typically public and therefore the type of information students share should be carefully considered.

Wikis

A wiki is a web-based collaborative writing environment that tracks the history of the document as it emerges. Although wikis tend to be used collaboratively, because the software tracks each contribution, assessment techniques can be both group and individual. Peer assessment methods can be used in addition to the teacher's assessment of the group's final product.

TRENDS IN ONLINE TECHNOLOGIES

A further category of tools that promote online participation are variously called social networking tools and include: social bookmarking, social networking (e.g., Facebook and MySpace), mashups, RSS feeds, YouTube, photo sharing, and podcasts. The strength of these tools is that they provide an online environment in which students can create their own content. Students might participate in a group to produce a podcast or they might work together to build a list of bookmarks using Delicious (social bookmarking). In this case, assessment might involve assessing both the product and the process.

ASSESSMENT OF ONLINE PARTICIPATION

Methods for assessing online participation vary with the type of technology, the task, and the desired outcome. Further, assessing online participation should not necessarily translate into assigning a grade; rather, the use of a mixture of both formal and informal assessment techniques is ideal. When determining whether to attach a grade (formal assessment), it is important to look at the goals and objectives of what is being assessed to establish whether a grade is necessary to achieve these purposes. Before deciding whether to use formal or informal techniques, consider the following questions:

1. **Who:** Will students be assessed individually or as a group? For example, if a student is graded on their own contributions, they may perceive responding to other students' comments as having less value.

2. **What:** What is valued—the substance of the contribution or the mere fact that a student posted? This is tied to the age-old question of process versus product.

3. **Where:** This question relates to where online participation will take place (i.e., which technology will be used). Is the technology easy to access for all? Is it a familiar environment?

4. **When:** This question relates to whether the online participation will be asynchronous or synchronous, and from there, how

often will the student be graded (e.g., by each posting, or each week, etc.).

5. **Why:** This is a critical question, why assess the online partici- pation? The response to this question will help determine whether the assessment should be formal or informal. Is the ac- tivity being assessed to encourage participation? Is the activity important to help the students learn more deeply? Is participa- tion aimed at community building?

6. **How:** It is critical that assessment be transparent and that stu- dents be informed as to how they will be assessed. Instructors can create rubrics or provide descriptions of how assessment will take place. The assessment criteria used should be public, whether within the online environment itself or on the course syllabus.

ASSESSMENT CRITERIA

Frameworks or grading rubrics are useful for planning and for assessing on- line participation. Students may also find the rubric useful as a guide for their own participation. In this section, we review four general criteria that are used to assess online participation. Considering these criteria can also help to clarify the goals and objectives of an online activity. Therefore, the best time to create an assessment rubric is before the course begins.

Quantity of Participation

Within online environments, it is often advisable to provide students with guidelines outlining the quantity of participation expected of them in a particular activity. Quantity can be measured in a variety of ways, depend- ing on your learning goals and the particular technology you are using. In a discussion board, for example, you can suggest that students must log in and post a minimum number of times per week. In a wiki, you might re- quire that students make a minimum number of contributions (original or edits of existing content). In a blog, students can be asked to submit one post per week.

Assessing the quantity of participation can be critical in ensuring that students establish regular and frequent engagement in an online activity. When assessing online participation, students appreciate tangible mea- sures, and quantity is an indicator of participation that students can readily gauge.

Measures of quantity can include: length of posts, number of contributions in a time period, overall contributions, and contributions of a certain type (e.g., comments, posts, edits in a wiki, etc.).

Recommendations:

1. Quantity requirements are important for encouraging participation that is regular and frequent; however, it should not be the only criteria used for assessing online participation. A student can contribute in terms of quantity without enhancing the online activity. Therefore, quantity should be used with assessment criteria that evaluate quality.

2. You can vary the quantity requirements across the duration of the course, assigning groups to take responsibility for contributing more during a scheduled week.

3. Participating online is generally time consuming. Therefore, quantity requirements should be in line with the weight you assign the activity in the final grade.

4. If you are assessing participation in an online discussion forum, some software packages will provide you with useful statistics not only about how many posts each student makes but how many posts students have read. If you can obtain these kinds of course statistics, then the criteria of quantity can apply to both writing and reading.

Quality of Written Communication

There is some debate about the pros and cons of assessing the quality of written communication. In some online environments, particularly where synchronous technologies such as chat are used, insisting on correct grammar and spelling might pose a barrier for those students that require extra time for reading and writing. On the other hand, you may have an online activity in which students are expected to communicate using a more formal academic style of writing. In that case, the quality of written communication might be an important assessment criterion.

Recommendations:

1. Even if writing standards are relaxed and are not being assessed, it is a good idea to inform students about your expected

standards of quality. All students will feel more comfortable participating online if they understand the appropriate level of etiquette, spelling, grammar, and formality expected for the course or activity.

2. A rubric might be helpful for students to understand how the quality of their contribution is determined. This could be a group activity, wherein the students help create a rubric, or one can be assigned.

3. Consider providing examples or even modeling the qualities being assessed. A common example in online discussion forums is to remind students that a post that just indicates agreement (i.e., "I agree") as a response is not sufficient to sustain a substantial online discussion.

Evidence of Skills and Knowledge (Learning)

Online participation enhances student learning in relation to course goals and outcomes. Students can demonstrate that they are learning within the course by referring to course readings when participating in online activities, contributing substantively to online discussions, building on the ideas of their peers, and ensuring that their participation meets your predetermined standards. Explicit guidelines describing what constitutes evidence of learning coupled with regular feedback is key to helping students to make the most of their online participation and ensures that assessment is consistent and fair.

Recommendations:

1. Provide students with grading frameworks or marking rubrics describing what you will be looking for as evidence that their participation in online activities is leading to course-related learning. With explicit guidelines, assessment is fair and consistent, and grading can be more systematic and objective.

2. Workload can be an important consideration when assessing student participation in online activities. Students can produce a large number of notes, posts, or wiki edits, depending on the activity. Can you scan posts for content or will you have to read every word? Can you ask students to assess their own learning in the form of a final reflection? Is a group grade appropriate? Planning ahead can make assessment manageable.

3. If students are new to the online environment, they can benefit from occasional encouragement, particularly early in the course or activity. This can be done through feedback and modeling.

4. Student peer or self-assessment of learning is a growing trend in the assessment of online participation. With peer or self-assessment, a clear grading rubric is important.

Contribution to the Building and Sustaining of a Learning Community

Online participation is rarely individual. Whether using a synchronous tool like chat or an asynchronous environment like a discussion board, student collaboration is often integral to the learning task. Therefore, making students' collaborative or teamwork skills part of assessment is important, as it indicates the significance of being a good group member.

Through assessment frameworks and rubrics, students can be encouraged to include others in discussion, foster equal participation, contribute regularly, and communicate with the aim of creating a supportive, friendly, and inclusive environment (University of Adelaide 2008). Think about what you would like to see demonstrated for assessment purposes. For example, a wiki can be used for collaborative group work, and the history of the final document can be used to gauge individual contributions. A chat tool used by a group to plan their project can be set to store a transcript of the discussion.

Recommendations:

1. Being explicit within the assessment framework and then modeling inclusive and supportive communication can be important in establishing and maintaining an environment in which students feel welcome to participate.

2. If teamwork or group work is part of an online activity, students can take on different roles, such as facilitator, moderator, or summarizer. Specific guidelines describing what will be expected for each role and how that participation will be assessed helps students to understand and meet expectations.

3. A combination of peer and instructor assessment of individual and group work can be used. Providing students with an oppor-

tunity to assess their peer's level of online participation can support the overall grade for a particular activity (Palloff and Pratt 2005).

CONCLUSION

Assessing online participation should be a transparent process for the student—they should know from the beginning of the course if they are to be formally or informally assessed and on what criteria that assessment will be based. This ensures that the students and the instructor have a shared understanding of what is expected within the course and of the value placed on online participation. It is our experience that instructors who do not place value (course credit) on online participation may find students less willing to engage, given other competing demands for their time. Assessing online participation provides recognition that the students' contributions are valued and that their participation contributes to the overall success of the course. See the "For Further Reflection and Action" section at the end of the book for more ideas on online participation assessment.

REFERENCES

Palloff, Rena M., and Keith Pratt. 2005. *Collaborating online: Learning together in community*. San Francisco: Jossey-Bass.

University of Adelaide. 2008. *Effective learning*. Http://www.adelaide.edu.au/clpd/online/assessonline/effectivelrng (accessed June 12, 2008).

When Learning Matters

Student Assessment Using Portfolios in Higher Education

Mercedes Rowinsky-Geurts
Wilfrid Laurier University

Professors have been impacted with an increased number of students. This increase has had a repercussion on the level of the students' participation and involvement in the learning process and has consequently forced professors to change their evaluation tools. One of the main concerns has to do with both the amount of time that grading will entail in a course and also with the assimilation of the material presented in the course. While developing a new film course on Spanish and Latin American filmmakers, I found myself contemplating the idea of including portfolios as an assessment tool. They would represent 40 percent of the final grade. The other 60 percent was divided as follows:

- In class tests (2)   20 % (10 % each)
- Film discussions   10 %
- Critical work (peer review) 20 %
- Tutorial attendance   10 %

The definition of a portfolio that I use is, "A purposeful collection of a student's work, often with samples of work collected over time and with reflections about what was learned or what a piece is supposed to demonstrate" as cited by Brookhart (1999, 55; also Arter, Spandel, and Culham 1995; Nitko 1996). One of the main goals of using portfolios is to focus on helping students become effective thinkers, as cited by Cameron (1999, in Stark et al. 1990). In order to accomplish such a goal, I follow Cameron's idea that students need to actively participate in the learning process. She states that: "Active learning asks that students use content knowledge, not just acquire it" (1999, 9). Another goal to keep in mind when using portfolios is the involvement of students not only with the material at hand, but also with their peers. Instead of focusing on their individual work, the portfolios allow students to give formative feedback to a peer, establishing a connection between members of the class rarely found in higher education.

The inclusion of portfolios used in this manner imposes great demands on both students and the instructor. The outcome was unknown to me, as this initiative was the first of its kind in any of my courses. I was apprehensive at first, but at the same time I felt a sense of confidence following a workshop on portfolios presented by Cynthia Weston at the Society for Teaching and Learning in Higher Education (STLHE) Conference in 2002. This article explores the use of portfolios as an evaluating tool focused on improving student learning and enhancing classroom participation.

It is crucial to present clear guidelines and specific goals to students with high expectations. If portfolios are going to be included, the evaluating process, tools, and expectations have to be clearly stated in the course outline so in case of doubts or concerns, students can access the information quickly. It is not conducive to structure the course methodology, approach, and evaluation considering that perhaps students will not respond to the challenge. Being afraid of their passivity will only restrain the possibilities of their learning (Kember and Wong 2000).

CLASS FORMAT

The class meets five hours[1] per week for twelve weeks, twice a week. The course is structured in such a manner that the full twelve weeks are needed in order to complete it. Class starts in the first meeting, where students are given a course outline, thirteen pages in length, including a clear explanation of the requirements for the course, followed by a prescreening lecture and a screening of the first film. The five hours a week are divided as follows:

- **Class One:** One hour prescreening lecture, followed by two hours for screening the film
- **Class Two:** One hour postscreening lecture, followed by two hours of tutorials with the instructor in which the class is divided in two groups to facilitate discussion. For the first six weeks, Group A attends tutorial 1, while Group B attends tutorial 2. At midcourse, the groups switch tutorials.

The course outline contains a clear and extensive explanation of what a portfolio entails, as well as a rubric for formative feedback (Table 1). Students are asked to pair up with a peer for evaluation purposes while they work on the portfolio. This last aspect is essential because students usually do not get to know their fellow classmates or their work. The exchange of assignments while providing and receiving formative feedback offers students an enriching learning experience. It is also educational for students to encounter a classroom environment like this one where people from different faculties are taking the same course. Such diversity offers students the possibility to discuss topics while they develop the ability to apply principles studied in their own disciplines. Topics from the films are discussed during tutorials, and life experiences and views about sensitive issues are explored in a safe and respectful manner. The fact that students know some of the opinions of at least one peer through the peer review process helps to open up the channels of communication. Hounsell and colleagues explain that "by opening up opportunities for students to acquaint themselves with one another's work at first hand, and so help to develop a common understanding of what has—and can be—achieved" (2008, 56). The first step has been taken by having the possibility of reading someone else's work in the class. In a way, they feel more comfortable sharing their own ideas compared to a group that haven't had the chance to explore their peers' work.

THE PROCESS: FOCUSING ON ACTIVE LEARNING

The way the portfolio works is as follows:

1. Students write a two-page analysis of the weekly film, focusing on a specific topic of the many presented in the *Assignment Guideline*. Topics such as characterization and plot, sights and sounds, edited images, sound, and viewer responses may be selected.

2. Upon completion, they pass it along to the selected peer.

3. Following the rubric for *Formative Feedback* presented in the course outline, each student offers comments to the chosen peer; the review itself represents twenty percent of the final grade. Students are evaluated twice on each piece: their own work and their evaluation of their peer.

4. Revised work with the peer's formative feedback is returned to the author, who can accept the comments of the peer and

	LEVEL OF ACHIEVEMENT		
CRITERION	OUTSTANDING	COMPETENT	REQUIRES RETHINKING
Mastery of Subject Matter	Consistent and sophisticated use of vocabulary and concepts	Appropriate vocabulary and concepts are used most of the time	Vocabulary and concepts are used inconsistently and may be inappropriate
	Extracts and applies all essential principles from readings	Many principles from readings recognized	A few principles from readings are recognized; some misinterpretations
	All components of the assignment executed with precision; no flaws or misinterpretations	Most components of evaluation design competently executed; some minor flaws	Major flaws or misinterpretation are apparent
	Sophisticated and appropriate links made between assignments and course readings	Links to course readings are appropriate but are limited	Links to course readings are absent or inappropriate
Coherence/ Alignment	Coherence/alignment maintained among all the concepts presented	Coherence/alignment maintained among most of the elements of the assignment; some minor flaws	Coherence/alignment among the ideas in the assignment not present
	Portfolio is a cohesive representation of work in which you have documented and assessed your development	Portfolio connects assignments, though development and progression not fully apparent	Portfolio is a series of disconnected assignments; linking and progression not apparent

Table 1. Criteria and Standards for Grading

	LEVEL OF ACHIEVEMENT		
CRITERION	OUTSTANDING	COMPETENT	REQUIRES RETHINKING
Explication	Rationales demonstrate a grasp of complexities and interrelationships among issues	Rationales are stated and are based on readings	Rationales may not be present, or based on an individual perspective
	Fully develops and communicates thinking behind all decisions, revisions, and rationales	Thinking is briefly expressed for most decisions and rationales	Thinking behind decisions and rationales is unexpressed or faulty
	Significance of decisions, revisions, and results is thoroughly analyzed and communicated	Significance is stated but analysis is minimal	Significance is neither recognized or not stated
Formative Approach	Exhibits a general drive to learn and improve by seeking and encouraging feedback in all activities	Readily receives and incorporates feedback to improve assignment	Documents experiences by describing or summarizing what happened
	Takes risks in assignment development	Takes a safe approach to develop the assignment	Progressions/connections are not detected
	Consistent, thoughtful, thorough completion of assignments, thus fully prepared for peer feedback	Own work usually completed thus adequately prepared for peer feedback	Conclusions may be poorly stated or not stated and may no refer to assignments

Table 1. Criteria and Standards for Grading (cont.)

	LEVEL OF ACHIEVEMENT		
CRITERION	OUTSTANDING	COMPETENT	REQUIRES RETHINKING
	Gives sensitive, essential feedback that enhances and encourages the work of others	Gives constructive feedback that identifies relevant issues for revision	
Organization	Assignments and portfolio are clearly structured and sequenced	Structure of assignments and portfolio is generally apparent with a few unclear moments	Structure of assignments or portfolio is muddled
	Appropriate headings and labels make pieces easy to locate	Some headings and labels may be missing or misplaced	Headings and labels are generally missing, misplaced, or poorly positioned
Language and Writing Style	Ideas are expressed logically and clearly so meaning is easy to comprehend	Some errors in usage, grammar, spelling, or punctuation, but meaning is clear	Multiple errors in usage, grammar, and punctuation interfere with meaning

Table 1. Criteria and Standards for Grading (cont.)

makes the necessary changes. Every three weeks, students hand in the portfolio to the instructor for *Formative Feedback* following the same rubric. That means that every three weeks, the instructor receives sixteen pages from each student who has analyzed three films. For each film they have prepared the following:

- Two pages for the first draft
- One page of comments from a peer
- Two pages for the revised draft
- One page of overall personal reflection—this piece is vital because students have the opportunity to express per-

sonal comments about the actual learning process to the instructor

5. With each submission to the instructor, students provide a one-page *Reflection* on the learning process. The instructor writes a response on the reflection, but no actual grade is given. The inclusion or absence of this portion of the portfolio is reflected in the category of *Quality and Completeness* of the portfolio. In the case that this section is not included, the instructor mentions its absence in the formative feedback and the student can complete it afterward.

6. Holistic grading is applied throughout the process. No grades are assigned until the end, but students have a clear understanding of what is expected of them. Improvement is ongoing, and students need to present all the versions clearly marked:

- Draft 1
  - Formative feedback from peer
- Draft 2
  - Formative feedback from instructor
  - Final version and the Reflection for each submission

7. At the end of the process, students have to set up a meeting with the instructor to discuss the grade they believe they deserve, as well as the one assigned to them. Even after this meeting, they could have another week to revise their work. Most of the time, no further revision is needed. These steps are important to foster students' learning and to develop their ability to think creatively and critically. At the same time, it gives students time to develop their skills incorporating the reading materials into their analysis. Such steps do not occur when grades are assigned to students' work with no further possibility for revisions.

ASSESSMENT FOCUSED ON LEARNING AND INVOLVEMENT

Often, students are required to provide instructors with individual work that is created in an isolated manner. Competitiveness for grades is alive and well in our institutions, and instead of students focusing on learning, they focus on performance, probably forgetting most of the material afterward. Using peer reviews in this way results in one of the most rewarding teaching and learning experiences. Students have consistently reported that this process offers them the opportunity to read their peers' work. They appreciate their remarks and often comment how much they had gained by exchanging their work with a colleague.

Peer review is done following the rubric presented in the outline—it is the same rubric used by the instructor; in this manner, no negative comments or hurtful remarks ever appear in the revisions. The detailed formative feedback rubric, based on the Cynthia Weston handout, is presented to students.

Such detailed information needs to be provided in order to avoid confusion when students compare pieces (Arter, Spandel, and Culham 1995) as cited by Brookhart (1999). In this manner, students have a clear idea of where the flaws are—if any—and they can easily execute the changes needed if they so prefer. The autonomy for improvement is solely in the students' hands, which empowers them. Tan explains that: "greater student involvement in assessment translates directly into greater student empowerment" (2008, 16). Students feel that because no final grade is given throughout the process, the motivation to improve the pieces is always present. This approach to learning is fundamentally different to the use of assigned work for which a grade is given and no further changes are permitted upon receiving the work back from the instructor.

Using portfolios in this manner promotes critical thinking, reflection about the learning process, and creates an invaluable sense of community within the class. Students have the time to go over their work, reflect on the ideas presented, consider the comments offered by their peer and the instructor, and proceed to change their work accordingly. This is one of the main strengths of using portfolios. Students report an increased proficiency in the topics studied, as well as a clear improvement in their writing skills. They are also appreciative of the fact that at the beginning of the course including material from the assigned readings in their analysis is difficult, but as the course progresses, the intertwining of reading materials within their analysis became easier and the assignments resulted in stronger pieces.

It is also significant to point out that due to the rigorous structure of the course, students are prepared for each meeting having done the readings and film analysis. They show an easier time communicating ideas in tutorials, increasing both class participation and developing a sense of commitment to personal achievement.

TIME AND PLANNING

As students learn that the portfolio is a place where learning takes place, they become very attached to them. They can see their progress. When comparing first and last pieces, they comment on how much they appreciate the ever-evolving learning process, and they put emphasis on how much they seem to notice their increased involvement with the course material.

Color coding of the various sections is recommended, and a clear and updated table of contents needs to be maintained at all times. Some instructors may think that all these demands could result in somewhat negative reactions from students, but students have consistently showed their dedication in creating high-quality portfolios. The neatness of the presentation, the attention to detail, and the care they invest in the process makes the actual portfolio something that students are proud of. The time that goes into handing in the best work possible, together with the fact that improvements can always occur throughout the process, becomes an incentive to develop their work. This assessment tool can be applied across all disciplines and levels.

Since time is of the essence for the process to work well, students are given clear dates for the portfolio's submissions. Restrictions and penalties regarding submission dates and times need to be strict. Students consistently hand in their work ahead of time. Some of them even do so the day before the deadline. As motivated as they are to hand in the portfolios, they are also keen to pick them up after the instructor's formative feedback is completed. Obviously, this puts a lot of stress on the instructor, but because students have shown such enthusiasm, the reward of reviewing their work becomes a pleasant adventure more than a task. It is a journey of discovery and learning in which both students and instructors embark. In order for the process to work, all those involved need to be respectful of the time constraints. For this goal to be achieved, students need to work on planning ahead. The peer reviewers must have their work done on time in order for their colleague to be able to do the revisions, complete the reflection, and update the table of contents for each submission (Figure 1).

LISTENING TO STUDENTS' CUES

The response to this method of assessment has proven successful. Students are not afraid of challenging assignments. In this half-credit course,

Figure 1. Typical path and evolution of portfolio development.

they actually express to have worked harder than for many of their full-credit courses or any other half-credit course. They experience a high level of reflection, not only on their own work but also on their peers' work, producing a higher level of assimilation of the material and actually applying some of the knowledge acquired in the course in some of their other courses. They have also shown a keen understanding of the topics and a higher level of class participation. At the same time, a deep sense of community, empathy, and solidarity is developed inside and outside the classroom. Following some of the screenings, students call each other to comment on the issues presented. They come to the lectures and tutorials prepared to share ideas and open up their minds to the views of others. More than anything else, the learning experience created with the use of the portfolio offers:

- A view of students' ideas
- The possibility for the instructor to address students' shortcomings and allow time to solve them
- The chance for students to read peers' work
- The opportunity for students to experience providing formative feedback
- An increase in students' participation
- Improvement in the quality of the final product
- Enhancement of student learning

Remember that most students have not experienced the need to systematically plan their work, so they will need reminders about the timelines. After the first submission, they quickly learn that they need to develop a keen understanding about the requirements of the course. Most of the learning experiences acquired with the use of the portfolio are proven to be successful and transferable skills students find valuable in the future.

NOTE

1. The students attend five hours per week, but the instructor's time is six hours per week.

REFERENCES

Arter, Judith A., Vicki Spandel, and Ruth Culham. 1995. Portfolios for assessment and instruction. *ERIC Digest*. ED 388 890. 4 pp. MF-01; PC-01. Http://ericae.net/db/ edo/ED388890.htm.

Brookhart, Susan M. 1999. The art and science of classroom assessment: The missing part of pedagogy. *ASHE-ERIC Higher Education Report 27* (1). Washington, DC: George Washington University, Graduate School of Education and Human Development.

Cameron, Beverly J. 1999. *Active learning*. Green Guide No. 2. Halifax, Nova Scotia, Canada: Society for Teaching and Learning in Higher Education (STLHE).

Hounsell, Dai, Velda Mccune, Jenny Hounsell, and Judith Ltjens. 2008. The quality of guidance and feedback to students. *Higher Education Research and Development*, *27*(1): 55–67.

Kember, David, and Anthony Wong. 2000. Implications for evaluation from a study of students' perceptions of good and poor teaching. *Higher Education, 40*(1): 60–97.

Nitko, Anthony J. 1996. *Educational assessment of students*. 2nd ed. Englewood Cliffs, NJ: Merrill.

Stark, Joan S., Malcolm A. Lowther, Richard J. Bentley, Michael P. Ryan, Gretchen G. Martens, Michele Genthon, Patricia A. Wren, and Kathleen M. Shaw. 1990. *Planning introductory college courses: Influences on faculty*. Ann Arbor: University of Michigan, National Center for Research to Improve Postsecondary Teaching and Learning.

Tan, Kelvin H. K. 2008. Qualitatively different ways of experiencing student self-assessment. *Higher Education Research and Development*, *27*(1): 15–29.

Conclusion

The objective of *Engaging Students* was to help faculty members and teachers transform students from passive to active learners. We looked at what it takes to prepare the ground for active participation. We also examined the necessary environment created to foster such engagement: conventional or virtual. A long article was devoted to the new technologies that appeal to twenty-first-century students: blogging, clickers, and podcasting are here to stay, and the articles on these topics provided the reader with some practical information, as well as some evidence of success. Finally, we explored different ways for assessing online and in-class participation.

In many ways, *Engaging Students* is a practical tool. For some readers, the articles probably confirmed what they already know and may have tried, but it is certainly my hope that this collection of articles has offered most readers the opportunity to reflect on their own teaching practices, and has given them the desire to experiment with new approaches with the confidence that others have used them with success.

I would like to leave the readers with a final quote that summarizes what *Engaging Students* is all about: "Teaching is challenging, exciting, maddening, absorbing—and potentially joyful. Every day, you have the opportunity to reach into the minds of your students and help them mature as learners."[1] The door is open, let the challenge begin!

NOTE

1. The Gwenna Moss Centre for Teaching Effectiveness, from their Web site for a course, Transforming Teaching, at http://www.usask.ca/gmcte/drupal/?q=transforming_teaching.

For Further Reflection and Action

Several of the authors in *Engaging Students* have provided additional suggestions for incorporating the ideas presented in their articles. For the convenience of the reader, they are gathered here.

From "Strategies for Engaging Students with Learning Disabilities," by Jacqueline A. Specht

1. How do you react to the idea of having students with learning disabilities in your class? How might these reactions influence your rapport with these students?

2. Do you have a center for students with disabilities on your campus? If you don't know, how could you find out? If you do, are you familiar with their process for working with students with disabilities?

3. Take the nine principles of universal design and recreate a lesson with them in mind. How many were you able to incorporate? Which ones did you find particularly easy or hard to incorporate? How might you get help with those that you found difficult? Do you think using these principles will affect the engagement of students? Why or why not?

From "The Inquiry Circle," by Jeanette McDonald

Don't be afraid to experiment, start small and decide how much risk to take on and the level of control you feel comfortable sharing with students. Think of the IC on a continuum where you move up and down with respect to the level of risk, shared control, and complexity of learning task. To help you visualize where you sit on the IC continuum for a given course, draw a line and mark an *X* where you feel most comfortable. Revisit your decision each time you offer the course.

From "Blog or Discussion Board: Which Is the Right Tool to Choose?" by Matt Crosslin

1. Have you ever used a blog or discussion board in your class? Did you use it for one of the incorrect usages discussed in this article? If so, do you agree with the analysis of why that usage was wrong? Why or why not?

2. Consider one of your class activities that you would like see expanded outside of class time. Which tool would be better for that activity—a blog or a discussion board? How would you set up that activity in the tool you have chosen?

3. Think of one way to use a blog and a discussion board in your class. Create one teacher-led activity for each tool and one student-led activity for each tool.

From "Broadcollecting: Using Personal Response Systems ('Clickers') to Transform Classroom Interaction," by Tom Haffie

1. When, during lectures as you currently offer them, do you ask questions to the class? What is the function of these questions?

2. Do you find that class participation is limited to only a few students? Are they representative of the class as a whole?

3. In what way would it be helpful to have immediate feedback on the learning that is occurring in response to your teaching?

4. How might regular feedback on their understanding be helpful for your students?

5. When could your preferred learning outcomes be served by active engagement activities, such as peer discussion?

From "Assessment of Online Participation" by Denise Stockley and Wendy Freeman

1. Think about what participation assessment techniques you have used in the past (if any), how successful they were, and whether you can adapt these strategies to the online environment? If yes, how? If no, why not?

2. Have you ever created an online activity and students did participate? Why do you think they participated? Conversely, have you ever created an online activity and students did not participate? Why do you think they didn't participate? What measures did you take the next time you taught the course to ensure this didn't happen again?

3. Do you use any of Stockley and Freeman's assessment criteria: (1) quantity, (2) quality, (3) evidence of skills and knowledge, and (4) contribution to the learning community? Are these criteria important to your approach to assessing online participation? Are there other criteria that you would add to this list?

4. Do you think the strategies offered in the chapter to assess online participation will encourage your students to participate online? Why or why not?

5. Stockley and Freeman advocate the importance of being transparent in your assessment of online participation (i.e., letting students know how and what will be assessed). What strategies have you used or will you employ to keep students informed?

List of Contributors

Philip C. Abrami, Ph.D. Centre for the Study of Learning and Performance, Concordia University, Montréal, Québec

Margaret D. Anderson, Ph.D. Psychology Department, State University of New York at Cortland, New York

Mike Atkinson, Ph.D. Department of Psychology, Dalhousie University, Halifax, St. Catherine's, Ontario

Ernest Biktimirov, Ph.D. Department of Finance and Operation Systems, Brock University, St Catherine's, Ontario

Kathy Cawsey, Ph.D. English Department, Dalhousie University, Halifax, Nova Scotia

Matt Crosslin, M.Ed. University of Texas at Arlington's Center for Distance Education, Arlington, Texas

Wendy Freeman, Ph.D. Department of Professional Communication, Ryerson University, Toronto, Ontario

Tom Haffie, Ph.D. Biology Department, University of Western Ontario, London, Ontario

Einat Idan. Centre for the Study of Learning and Performance, Concordia University, Montréal, Québec

Jeanette McDonald, Ph.D. (ABD) Educational Development, Wilfrid Laurier University, Waterloo, Ontario

Elizabeth Meyer, Ph.D. Centre for the Study of Learning and Performance, Concordia University, Montréal, Québec

Vanitha Pillay, M.Ed. Centre for the Study of Learning and Performance, Concordia University, Montréal, Québec

M. Louise Ripley, M.B.A., Ph.D. Atkinson Faculty of Professional and Liberal Studies, York University, Toronto, Ontario

Mercedes Rowinsky-Geurts, Ph.D. Department of Languages and Literatures, Wilfrid Laurier University, Ontario

Jacqueline A. Specht, Ph.D. Faculty of Education, University of Western Ontario, London, Ontario

Denise Stockley, Ph.D. Centre for Teaching and Learning, Queen's University, Kingston, Ontario

Anne Wade, M.L.I.S. Centre for the Study of Learning and Performance, Concordia University, Montréal, Québec

Eileen Wood, Ph.D. Psychology Department, Wilfrid Laurier University, Waterloo, Ontario

Dave Yearwood, Ph.D., C.S.I.T. Technology Department, University of North Dakota, Grand Forks, North Dakota

Index

About the Author

Catherine Black, an Associate Professor of French, recently arrived at Simon Fraser University (British Columbia), has been teaching for 20 years in two other Canadian universities (the University of Waterloo and Wilfrid Laurier University). She has been awarded multiple teaching and leadership awards. For several years, she was a Faculty Associate for Instructional Development and a mentor for new faculty members. In this capacity, she has advised, in dozens of workshops, many new and more senior colleagues, as well as future instructors (PH.D and MA candidates) on pedagogy, course design, and innovative teaching approaches.

She is also the co-author of two textbooks, and has presented her research, which focuses on innovative teaching approaches designed to motivate students, at many national and international conferences.